∽ · ∽ · ∽

"Bartik has a gift for clear, straightforward exposition. This new book makes a comprehensive and compelling case for a strong public commitment to early childhood education."
—*Nancy Folbre, University of Massachusetts–Amherst, and author of* Valuing Children: Rethinking the Economics of the Family

"*From Preschool to Prosperity* is an enormously useful book that merits wide circulation. It does a great job of synthesizing, and the proposal makes educational sense."
—*David Kirp, University of California, Berkeley, and author of* Kids First

"A wise and thoughtful exposition of why we should invest in early childhood education. Bartik does an excellent job of debunking some common myths."
—*William Gormley, Georgetown University, and author of* Voices for Our Children

"The economic benefits of investing in high-quality early childhood education are clear and backed by an impressive amount of research, as laid out in Tim Bartik's book. With businesses concerned about securing a future skilled workforce, with our military leaders concerned about the future supply of qualified recruits, and with our society concerned about the troubling increase in income inequality, we should be looking at proven investments in children and youth that strengthen our human capital and the future of our economy."
—*Arthur J. Rolnick, University of Minnesota; former Senior Vice President and Director of Research, Federal Reserve Bank of Minneapolis*

"Early childhood education is among the best investments we can make as a country. Timothy Bartik explains why with hardheaded and clear analysis. He makes a compelling case for business leaders to engage in their communities to ensure we properly invest in the future of our youth."
—*Lenny Mendonca, Director Emeritus, McKinsey and Company*

"There is no product the U.S. economy produces that is more important than ready-for-life 18-year-olds. Without them there is no future workforce or an economy! Business people are beginning to understand this. In his second extraordinary book on early childhood, Tim Bartik explains how early learning investment can strengthen the national economy and address economic inequality by increasing economic opportunity. Are there today any two economic topics more crucial than these? A must-read for business leaders worldwide."
—*Robert Dugger, Managing Partner, Hanover Provident Capital*

∽ · ∽ · ∽

From Preschool to Prosperity

From Preschool to Prosperity

The Economic Payoff to Early Childhood Education

Timothy J. Bartik

2014

W.E. Upjohn Institute for Employment Research
Kalamazoo, Michigan

Library of Congress Cataloging-in-Publication Data

Bartik, Timothy J.
  From preschool to prosperity : the economic payoff to early childhood education /
Timothy J. Bartik.
    pages cm. — (WE focus series)
  Includes bibliographical references and index.
    ISBN 978-0-88099-482-8 (pbk. : alk. paper) — ISBN 0-88099-482-7 (pbk. : alk.
paper)
    1. Early childhood education—Economic aspects—United States. 2. Education,
Preschool—Economic aspects—United States. 3. Early childhood education—United
States. 4. Education, Preschool—United States. I. Title.
    LB1139.25.B37 2014
    372.210973—dc23
                                          2014025597

© 2014
W.E. Upjohn Institute for Employment Research
300 S. Westnedge Avenue
Kalamazoo, Michigan 49007-4686

The facts presented in this study and the observations and viewpoints expressed are
the sole responsibility of the author. They do not necessarily represent positions of
the W.E. Upjohn Institute for Employment Research.

Cover design and illustrations by Simon Kalil Borst.
Index prepared by Diane Worden.
Printed in the United States of America.
Printed on recycled paper.

Contents

Acknowledgments   xi

Preface   xiii

1   Introduction   1
    What Are Early Childhood Education Programs?   2
    What Are the Benefits from Early Childhood Education?   4
    How Can Early Childhood Education Affect the Child's Future   5
        Life Course?
    A Proposal for Early Childhood Education   6
    The Plan of the Book   7

2   What Is the Evidence on the Earnings Effects of High-Quality   9
   Early Childhood Education, and Why Should We Believe It?
    Why the Research Evidence for Early Childhood Education   9
        Is Credible
    Random Assignment Studies   10
    Other Long-Term Studies with Good Comparison Groups: 11
        Head Start
    The Chicago Child-Parent Center Program   12
    Predicting Long-Term Earnings Effects from Short-Term Test   13
        Score Effects
    Infant Health and Development Program   15
    North Carolina's Smart Start Program, and More at Four   16
    State and Local Pre-K Programs: The Regression   17
        Discontinuity Evidence
    Summary of the Evidence   19

3   How Do the Adult Earnings Benefits of High-Quality Early   23
   Childhood Education Compare to Costs?
    Future Earnings versus Present Costs   23
    Parental Earnings   26
    Are These Effects Large?   26
    Closing Comments   27

4 Criticisms of the Research Evidence   29

    Criticism 1: The Evidence for Early Childhood Education's   29
       Benefits Only Comes from Small and Expensive Experiments
       Run a Long Time Ago

    Criticism 2: Early Childhood Education Is Argued to Be   31
       Ineffective because the Recent Head Start Experiment Has Test
       Score Effects That Quickly Faded to Statistical Insignificance

    Criticism 3: Why Haven't Oklahoma and Georgia, Two States   35
       That Have Prominently Adopted Universal Pre-K, Been More
       Obviously Successful in Improving Test Scores and Other
       Social Indicators?

    Criticism 4: The Recent Tennessee Pre-K Experiment Shows   37
       That Test Score Effects Quickly Fade, Which Raises Questions
       about whether State Pre-K Programs Are Effective

    Concluding Comments   39

5 How Can Early Childhood Education Programs Best Be   41
Designed?

    Quality of Teacher-Child Interactions   41
    Class Size and Teacher Credentials   42
    Middle-Class Children   44
    Program Duration   48
    Earlier versus Later Interventions   49

6 Spillover Benefits: How Does Early Childhood Education   53
Affect Other Groups Than Those Families Directly Served
by These Programs?

    Skill Spillovers   53
    Peer Effects in Education   56
    Spillovers from Reducing Crime   57
    Government/Taxpayer Benefits   58
    Pre-K: The Next Generation   59
    Concluding Comments   60

7 **A Proposed Early Childhood Education Strategy** 61
Full-Day Universal Pre-K for Four-Year-Olds 61
Targeted Educare/Abecedarian for All Disadvantaged Children 63
Nurse Family Partnership for All Disadvantaged First-Time 64
   Mothers
Costs 64
Aggregate Benefits 66
Accountability and Quality Improvement 68
What Level of Government Should Be Responsible for Early 69
   Childhood Education?
Concluding Comments 71

8 **Why Early Childhood Education Makes Sense Now: ECE's** 73
Place in the Ongoing Struggle for Broader Economic
Opportunities
Labor Supply and Labor Demand 73
History Matters 73
The Continuing Argument over Expanding Educational Access 74
But Why Early Childhood Education? And Why Now? 76
Doing the Good We Know How to Do 77

Notes 79

References 93

Author 103

Index 105

About the Institute 113

Figures

2.1 How Test Scores of Tulsa Pre-K Entrants and Former Pre-K Students 19
Vary with Age

3.1 Average Percentage Increase in Adult Earnings for Three Early Childhood 24
Education Programs

4.1 Predicted Percentage Effects on Adult Earnings of Early Childhood 33
Programs, Based on Test Scores versus Adult Outcomes

6.1 Effects of a 1 Percent Increase in Metro Workers Who Are College 55
Graduates on a Metro Area's Average Wages

Tables

2.1 Adult Earnings Effects, Compared with Predicted Earnings Effects 14
Based on Test Scores

3.1 Per-Child Earnings Benefits versus Costs of Three Early Childhood 25
Programs
5.1 How Earnings Benefits of Pre-K per Child Vary for Children from 47
Different Income Groups

7.1 Benefits versus Costs per Child of Adding Educare to Pre-K 63
7.2 Annual National Costs of Large-Scale Early Childhood Education Proposal 65

Acknowledgments

I greatly appreciate comments on a preliminary draft of this book by Laura Bornfreund, Susan Broman, Megan Carolan, Nancy Folbre, William Gormley, Rob Grunewald, Lisa Guernsey, Kevin Hollenbeck, Michelle Miller-Adams, Sandy Standish, Judy Temple, Sara Watson, Conor Williams, Jeff Woolston, and Tracy Zimmerman. These comments helped significantly sharpen and clarify the book, although I take full responsibility for the final book draft.

I thank Wei-Jang Huang and Linda Richer for research assistance, Claire Black for administrative and secretarial support, Ben Jones for editing, Erika Jackson for typesetting, Richard Wyrwa for publicity, and Simon Kalil Borst for his cover and cartoons. I thank all of those who provided a blurb for the book, as well as Sara Watson and Tony Shivers for their help in obtaining some of these blurbs. Finally, I appreciate the support for my research by my employer, the Upjohn Institute, and its president, Randy Eberts.

Preface

This book is my second book on preschool. My first book, *Investing in Kids: Early Childhood Programs and Local Economic Development* (2011), focused on exploring the connection between early childhood programs and the economic development of American states and metro areas, and in particular on comparing early childhood programs with business tax incentives.

Why a second book? Two reasons. First, the present book is much, much shorter, which I hope will mean it is more reader-friendly. Second, the present book is more focused on the key policy issues that today face early childhood education in the United States.

This book provides concise and research-based information to the following audiences:

- Professors looking for a review for their students of what research says about the effects of early childhood education;

- Members of the business community who want to see bottom-line figures on preschool's economic effects;

- Early childhood advocates who are puzzled about how to respond to common arguments given against early childhood education;

- Federal, state, or local administrators exploring ideas about how to better design and manage early childhood programs;

- Voters without preschool-aged children who might wonder, "What's my stake in this policy debate?";

- Federal, state, or local legislators who need to develop specific early childhood programs;

- Anyone interested in how early childhood programs might both boost American economic growth and reduce inequality.

My aim has been to make this book clear and accessible to a broad, nontechnical audience, while also giving readers the evidence and arguments they need to make up their own minds. Early childhood education is not just important to parents and preschool teachers; it is important to everyone interested in America's future prosperity. I hope this book contributes to the needed democratic debate, at all levels of government, over a possible significant expansion of early childhood education.

Checkmate already? Dangit, George, where the heck did you go to preschool?

Chapter 1

Introduction

W ouldn't it be great if there was some feasible policy that could boost the American economy and enlarge opportunities for more of our children?

We're in luck. Our economic future and our children's future can be significantly improved by expanding high-quality early childhood education programs, such as pre-K education.

In this book, early childhood education is examined from an economic perspective. The book evaluates the empirical evidence on the economic payoff to investing in early childhood education. What does this evidence imply for public policy?

An economic perspective includes quantifying the effects of early childhood education as benefits and costs measured in dollar terms. Although early childhood education programs have many benefits, this book will focus on one key benefit: earnings increases. Children who participate in high-quality early childhood education will tend to have higher earnings as adults, because these programs help unlock the child's potential for skills development.

An economic perspective includes comparing benefits with costs. Not all early childhood education programs are equal in their "bang for the buck."

An economic perspective includes examining who should pay for early childhood education programs. A key question is, "Who benefits from early childhood education?" Why should a taxpayer pay for other people's children? One reason is that early childhood education can do more than benefit former child participants. Early childhood education can have large spillover benefits for others in society, including other workers, families, state and local economies, and government budgets. These spillover benefits are sufficiently local to justify support for these programs by state and local governments.

But federal support may be helpful for program evaluation to ensure quality, and for early childhood programs targeted at the poor.

WHAT ARE EARLY CHILDHOOD EDUCATION PROGRAMS?

In this book, early childhood education programs include any publicly supported program that has as a principal purpose providing children younger than age five with educational services. The goal of such educational services is to improve the child's lifetime opportunities. Education is defined broadly to include cognitive skills as well as social or character skills. Early childhood education includes pre-K programs, parenting programs that provide parents with support in the art of parenting, and child care services with a strong educational component.

Early childhood education includes diverse programs. These programs can be targeted at children from disadvantaged families, or they can be more universal. (To avoid misinterpretation, let me state that "universal" programs are not compulsory. Rather, universal programs are available as an option for all families, without means-testing.) Early childhood education programs can be financed by federal, state, and local governments. These programs can be full-time from birth to age five, or they can operate for only one school year for a half-day at age four. Which approach will be the most cost-effective in increasing economic growth and expanding opportunities?

The book's focus is on how early childhood education can influence the child's future, and how that benefits society. But the book also considers benefits for parents. For example, child care frees up parent time for work or education.

Early childhood education includes diverse pre-K programs. Pre-K programs include the federally funded Head Start program, begun in 1965 as part of the War on Poverty. Head Start currently serves around one million children at a cost of around $8 billion. Pre-K programs include past experimental programs such as the Perry

Preschool Program, a 1960s program run by the HighScope Educational Research Foundation in Ypsilanti, Michigan, with follow-up data still being collected today. Pre-K programs also include many large-scale state and local pre-K programs. This includes Chicago's Child-Parent Center Program (CPC), as well as state-financed pre-K programs in more than 40 states. As of 2012–2013, state pre-K programs served 1.3 million children at an annual cost of over $6 billion.[1] State pre-K has expanded in the past decade: From 2002 to 2013, the percentage of all U.S. four-year-olds in state pre-K programs doubled, from 14 percent to 28 percent. Recently, state pre-K programs have faced cutbacks because of state fiscal problems.

Some state pre-K programs are close to universal. Oklahoma's pre-K program provides pre-K services to 74 percent of all four-year-olds in the state, with an additional 13 percent served by Head Start. Seven other states provide pre-K services to more than half of the state's four-year-olds: Florida, Vermont, Wisconsin, West Virginia, Iowa, Georgia, and Texas.

Recent proposals have been made to expand federal support for state pre-K programs. The short-term political outlook is that large-scale expansion of federal support is unlikely.[2]

Early childhood education includes programs to improve parenting. These parenting programs often operate through home visits, in which a trained visitor interacts at home with the parent and child. The most extensively evaluated of such home-visiting/parenting programs is the Nurse Family Partnership (NFP). The NFP involves nurses making home visits from the prenatal period up to age two to a disadvantaged first-time mom and her child. The NFP has expanded with the Affordable Care Act (ACA): The ACA authorized about $0.4 billion per year for research-proven home-visiting programs, including the NFP.

Early childhood education includes child care with a significant focus on the child's education. The most researched such program is the Abecedarian Project. This experiment, begun in North Carolina in 1972, provided five years of full-time educational child care and pre-K services for children from six weeks after birth to age five. More recently, a program similar to Abecedarian, called Educare, has been promoted around the United States by the Buffett Early Childhood Fund and the Ounce of Prevention Fund. This book's definition of early childhood education does not include subsidized child care programs that do not focus on education. For example, the Child Care and Development Fund, a federal block grant to states created by welfare reform, has such low funding per child and such weak quality screens that it clearly is not aimed at better child development.

WHAT ARE THE BENEFITS FROM EARLY CHILDHOOD EDUCATION?

The main direct benefit of early childhood education is the resulting improvement in the future life course of the child. The child's better life course is manifested in part by higher lifetime earnings. These earnings are valuable to the child. These earnings also mean the child is playing a more productive role in the American economy. And, these earnings enable the child to be more self-sufficient, a better husband or wife, a better parent, and a better contributor to neighborhood and civic life.

Greater legal earnings are accompanied by lower criminal activity. Lower costs of the criminal justice system and lower crime victimization are important social benefits of early childhood education.

A more fundamental spillover benefit of early childhood education is what it means for overall economic productivity. As explored in Chapter 6, when some workers gain more skills, wages increase for other workers. Businesses are more likely to invest in new technologies if average skills increase.

HOW CAN EARLY CHILDHOOD EDUCATION AFFECT THE CHILD'S FUTURE LIFE COURSE?

A skeptic could argue that no program that provides services for such a limited time—say a pre-K program for one school year at age four—could affect a child's future earnings at age 40. Government intervention could only work, a skeptic might say, by taking over the child's upbringing. Such a role is inappropriate for a government that respects individual liberty.

But, as explored in Chapter 2, the evidence suggests that even very time-limited early childhood education can have large effects on adult outcomes. This empirical evidence is surprising. Obviously it can't be that knowing a few more letters and numbers at kindergarten entrance influences adult earnings at age 40 by any direct effect. Somehow, what happens early to the child's development must have some indirect benefits for future development.

A plausible logic for long-term effects of early childhood education is as follows. The child's brain is more malleable prior to age five than in later years. Suppose an early childhood program increases the child's skills: cognitive skills such as math and reading skills; social skills such as getting along with peers and teachers; character skills such as patience, persistence, and self-confidence.

All of these skills prepare the child for later learning. The five-year-old with more skills will do better in kindergarten, interacting better with peers and the kindergarten teacher, and gaining further self-confidence. As a result of this greater learning in kindergarten, this child enters first grade better set up for further learning. And so on.

Early childhood education can develop skills that lead to more skills growth later. Early childhood education investment appreciates over time rather than depreciates. As Nobel Prize–winning economist James Heckman has said, "Skill begets skill" (Heckman 2000, p. 3).

The effect of any early childhood education program is relative to what would have happened without the program. Even without new early childhood education programs, there are existing public programs. In addition, most parents spend much time educating their child—for example, through talking and reading with their child and exposing the child to the natural world, playgrounds, museums, and the library. Parents may also spend money on private child care or pre-K. The benefits of any early childhood education program depend upon its superiority to what is already being provided by the public sector, or to what the parents are able to provide on their own. This means that the benefits of early childhood education may vary with the abilities or resources of the child's parents.

Parents may be unable to "go it alone" because early childhood education is often expensive. For example, high-quality full-day pre-K may cost over $10,000 per school year. Such a cost is difficult for even middle-class parents to afford.

As explored in Chapters 3 and 5, the benefit-cost analysis of early childhood education also depends on costs. The cost per child will tend to be higher at earlier ages, when class sizes will be lower.

Alternative services available to parents and higher costs are two reasons why the earliest possible interventions may not offer the highest ratio of benefits to costs. Brain neurons may indeed develop more at ages one and two; however, earlier intervention has a high opportunity cost, because it substitutes for something that many parents can provide on their own. Earlier intervention also has higher program costs per child, because younger children require more individual attention.

A PROPOSAL FOR EARLY CHILDHOOD EDUCATION

Based on this research, this book argues that we know enough to move forward with a full-scale proposal for early childhood education. This proposal has economic benefits exceeding costs, and it would particularly help children from poor and working-class families.

The proposal includes

- Universal full-day pre-K at age four for children from all income backgrounds;

- For low-income children, developmental child care and pre-K from birth to age five;

- For low-income families, home-visiting programs to improve parenting.

This proposal's national cost is $79 billion annually.[3] This cost is 2 percent of total government taxes.[4]

This proposal would not reverse all of the recent increases in U.S. income inequality since 1979, but it would help. For low-income Americans, this proposal would offset most of the increased income inequality since 1979; for middle-income Americans, this proposal would offset one-sixth of the increased income inequality (see Chapter 7).

THE PLAN OF THE BOOK

Chapter 2 summarizes the empirical evidence that has led most researchers to believe that early childhood programs can affect adult outcomes.

Chapter 3 compares adult earnings benefits from early childhood education with costs.

Chapter 4 analyzes common criticisms made of the empirical evidence for early childhood education.

Chapter 5 discusses how the benefits and costs of early childhood programs vary with program features, such as classroom quality, program duration, and the income of the child's family.

Chapter 6 explores social benefits of early childhood programs.

Chapter 7 outlines a specific early childhood proposal.

Chapter 8 puts early childhood education in the context of past efforts to reform American education.

In sum, this book argues the following:

- Many early childhood education programs have rigorous evidence for high benefit-cost ratios.

- We know something about what types of programs have the biggest bang for the buck, and how to improve program quality over time.

- Benefits of early childhood education are broad enough that taxpayer support is justified.

- Benefits of early childhood education are local enough to justify support by state and local governments.

- Early childhood education can play a significant role in an overall economic strategy to enhance U.S. economic growth and broaden economic opportunities.

Chapter 2

What Is the Evidence on the Earnings Effects of High-Quality Early Childhood Education, and Why Should We Believe It?

The empirical evidence is that high-quality early childhood education has large effects on a child's future adult earnings. Early childhood education can increase a child's future adult earnings by over 25 percent, and many programs have average future earnings effects of 3 percent or much greater. Over a career, even a 3 percent earnings boost amounts to many thousands of dollars.

But why should we believe this evidence? This chapter addresses this question.

WHY THE RESEARCH EVIDENCE FOR EARLY CHILDHOOD EDUCATION IS CREDIBLE

Why are the large benefit estimates for some early childhood programs believable? These estimates are believable because they come from rigorous research. Rigorous research means that the studies have good comparison groups. These comparison groups are made up of children similar to the children who participate in early childhood education, except for that participation. This comparability means that the estimated earnings increases are due to the program, not to preexisting differences between the program group and the comparison group.

Good comparison groups are needed because children are diverse. The child who participates in an early childhood education program may differ from the child who does not. Differences in observed child characteristics can be controlled for. We cannot control for differences in child characteristics that are unobserved. If we lack good comparison groups, post-program differences may be due to unobserved characteristics, not the program. Perhaps program children have more ambitious parents, which biases the study toward finding positive program effects. Alternatively, perhaps program children have more preexisting problems, which lead the parents to enroll their children in the program. These preexisting problems will bias the research toward finding negative program effects.

The problem of bad comparison groups is called selection bias. Families self-select into enrolling their children in early childhood education. The families who self-select may have children with different unobserved characteristics from those who do not.

Bias may also occur because of the program's selection procedures. The program may screen out children with too many problems, or it may enroll the neediest children. Outcome differences between the program and comparison groups may be due to this program selection.

RANDOM ASSIGNMENT STUDIES

How can research on early childhood education solve the selection bias problem? In some studies, the solution is that children are selected for the program using random assignment. Long-term effects of early childhood education are estimated in several well-done random assignment studies: Perry Preschool, the Abecedarian program, and the Nurse Family Partnership.

Perry was a half-day pre-K program at ages three and four in Ypsilanti, Michigan, from 1962 to 1967. The Abecedarian program was a full-time, full-year child care and pre-K program, from birth to age five, conducted from 1972 to 1977 in Chapel Hill, North Carolina. (The current Educare program is similar to Abecedarian.) The Nurse Family Partnership provides 2.5 years of nurse home visits to first-time mothers, from the prenatal period to age two. It has been subject to three experiments: 1) Elmira, New York (1977); 2) Memphis (1987); and 3) Denver (1994). The NFP is an ongoing program with many U.S. sites. Perry, Abecedarian, and the NFP were all targeted at disadvantaged families.

These experiments found large long-term benefits. Perry Preschool on average increased its child participants' future earnings by 19 percent. The Abecedarian program increased adult educational attainment and employment rates: The adult education effects predict a lifetime earnings increase of 15 percent. The higher adult employment rates, which exceed the boost expected from the educational attainment gains, bring the predicted lifetime earnings increase to 26 percent.[5] The Nurse Family Partnership increased school test scores and reduced crime. These effects predict an average increase in lifetime earnings of 3 percent.[6]

Random assignment is the gold standard for ensuring that estimated program effects are credible. Random assignment means that we would expect the "treatment" and "control" groups to have the same average level of unobserved characteristics. (The "treatment" group are the children randomly assigned to participate in the program; the "control" group are the children randomly assigned to not participate.) Any sizable difference in outcomes between the treatment and control groups is likely due to the "treatment" (the program participation), not to unobserved characteristics.[7]

OTHER LONG-TERM STUDIES WITH GOOD COMPARISON GROUPS: HEAD START

In addition to these small random assignment experiments, rigorous evidence for long-run effects of early childhood education comes from large-scale programs that are not random assignment experiments but that still have good comparison groups.[8] These studies have good comparison groups because they use data from natural experiments: natural accidents have resulted in similar persons having different access to early childhood education. Rigorous evidence for the long-term benefits of large-scale programs comes from studies of Head Start and of the Chicago Child-Parent Center Program.

Evidence on Head Start's long-term effects comes from two types of studies with good comparison groups. First, a study by Ludwig and Miller (2007) compares long-run outcomes for children in two different types of counties: 1) counties that adopted Head Start in its early years and 2) otherwise similar counties that did not. Ludwig and Miller focus on counties whose early participation in Head Start occurred because Head Start provided extra technical assistance to high-poverty counties to help them write a good Head Start application. This technical assistance boosted Head Start program activity in these counties, compared to similar counties that just missed the poverty cutoff.

Ludwig and Miller compare long-term outcomes for children in counties that just made the cutoff for Head Start technical assistance versus children in similar counties that just missed the cutoff. This is a good comparison group, as it is hard to think of any reason, other than the Head Start participation, that would lead to large differences in child outcomes in counties on either side of the cutoff. Ludwig and Miller found that children in counties that made the cutoff had lower mortality rates after Head Start was begun, and higher educational attainment later on.

Second, other Head Start studies compare siblings, one of whom participated in Head Start and the other of whom did not. This is a good comparison group because the comparison holds constant unobserved family characteristics.

A sibling comparison study by Garces, Thomas, and Currie (2002) suggests that Head Start increases educational attainment and reduces crime for some groups. Another sibling comparison study by Deming (2009) finds effects of Head Start on adult outcomes that predict an average earnings increase of 11 percent.

THE CHICAGO CHILD-PARENT CENTER PROGRAM

Evidence on the long-term effects of large-scale pre-K programs comes from studies of the Chicago Child-Parent Center Program

(CPC). This program, started in 1967 and run by the Chicago Public Schools, provides participants with from one to two years of half-day pre-K at ages three and four. About half of the children in CPC participated only at age four, and the other half at both ages three and four. Research on the CPC program uses as a comparison group children in similar neighborhoods in which the CPC program was not offered. This is a good comparison group because program participation depends on the accidents of geography, not on self-selection or program selection.[9]

CPC research has now followed former CPC participants, and the comparison group, through age 28. These results predict that CPC on average increases earnings by 8 percent.[10]

PREDICTING LONG-TERM EARNINGS EFFECTS FROM SHORT-TERM TEST SCORE EFFECTS

Direct evidence on the long-term earnings effects of early childhood education is better than indirect evidence. But long-term studies are scarce and expensive. Long-term studies also cannot produce results for more recent programs.

Long-term earnings effects can be predicted from a program's effects on test scores in the short term. Research by Chetty et al. (2011), Currie and Thomas (2012), and others has produced good evidence on how early test scores affect adult earnings.[11]

How good are such predictions? For early childhood education, early test-score effects tend to underpredict long-run earnings effects. Table 2.1 shows test score predictions and adult earnings effects for four early childhood programs.[12]

The initial post-program test scores tend to underpredict eventual adult earnings effects.[13] The third-grade test scores are even more of an underprediction of adult earnings effects. Possible reasons for this fading of results are discussed in Chapter 4. The bottom line is that test score predictions of adult earnings effects provide a conservative estimate of program benefits.

Table 2.1 Adult Earnings Effects, Compared with Predicted Earnings Effects Based on Test Scores

	Long-run earnings effects based on adult outcomes (% of adult earnings)	Predicted earnings effects based on end-of-program test scores (% of adult earnings)	Predicted earnings effects based on third-grade test scores (% of adult earnings)
Perry Preschool	19	12	2 to 5
Abecedarian	26	13	7 to 11
Chicago Child-Parent Center Pre-K	8	8	1
Head Start	11	3 to 6	1 to 3

NOTE: Adult earnings effects are shown as predicted average percentage increase in earnings due to the program, compared to expected earnings if the person had not participated in the program. End-of-program test scores are for the end of preschool or for kindergarten.

SOURCE: Author's calculations, as explained in text and endnotes.

Hundreds of studies of early childhood education programs have estimated test score effects. Analyses of this research have been done by Camilli et al. (2010) and Leak et al. (2010). Leak et al. find average short-term test score effects that predict adult earnings effects of 5 percent.[14] Camilli et al. find average test score effects that predict adult earnings effects of 9 percent.[15]

But the Camilli et al. and Leak et al. meta-analyses are not precise enough to guide policy. The average effects come from studies with diverse methodologies of variable quality, and the programs studied have different designs, costs, and quality.

This book will focus on a few of these studies that have particularly good comparison groups. These studies include the following three categories: 1) the Infant Health and Development Program; 2) North Carolina's Smart Start and More at Four programs; and 3) studies of state and local pre-K programs that have been done using regression discontinuity methods, which will be explained below.

INFANT HEALTH AND DEVELOPMENT PROGRAM

The Infant Health and Development Program (IHDP) was an experiment conducted from 1985 to 1988 at eight U.S. sites. The program provided high-quality full-time child care at ages one and two.[16] The program replicated features of the Abecedarian program. However, whereas the Abecedarian program provided full-time child care and pre-K from birth to age five, the IHDP only provided such services for two years.

The IHDP was a random assignment experiment. Duncan and Sojourner's (2013) analysis of these data suggest that for low-income children, the IHDP had many statistically significant and substantively large effects on test scores.[17] The third-grade test effects predict that the IHDP would on average boost adult earnings by 12 percent.[18]

NORTH CAROLINA'S SMART START PROGRAM, AND MORE AT FOUR

Smart Start is a state of North Carolina program, begun in 1993, that provides state aid to county partnerships that try to improve the quality of local early-childhood services, from birth to age four. Most Smart Start funds have been devoted to child care, including child care subsidies to low-income families and training for child care centers.

More at Four was a state of North Carolina program from 2001 to 2011 that supported full-day pre-K at age four. It has since been renamed NC Pre-K.

A recent study (Ladd, Muschkin, and Dodge 2014) relies on a natural experiment: Both Smart Start and More at Four were gradually rolled out to different counties. The researchers use this natural variation in funding by county and time period to estimate these programs' effects on third-grade test scores. This study has a good comparison group because it is unclear why third-grade test scores in different counties would change in response to lagged program funding except for a true program effect.

Based on Ladd et al.'s estimated test score effects, typical levels of Smart Start or More at Four funding are predicted to increase average future earnings in a county by 1.6 percent for Smart Start and by 2.9 percent for More at Four.[19] Over an entire career, a 1.6 percent earnings boost is a lot of money.

These average effects include many children who receive few or no services from these two programs. In the typical county, only 25 percent of four-year-olds participated in pre-K funded by More at Four, so it is remarkable that the program increases average earnings by 2.9 percent. Extrapolation implies that increasing a county's enrollment in More at Four from zero to 100 percent would boost earnings by over 11 percent. For Smart Start, average spending per child under the age of five is only $220 annually, so the 1.6 percent earnings effect is large compared to this cost.

STATE AND LOCAL PRE-K PROGRAMS:
THE REGRESSION DISCONTINUITY EVIDENCE

Rigorous evidence for large-scale state or local pre-K programs comes from studies that look at student performance on the same test at entrance to the pre-K program for four-year-olds and at entrance to kindergarten. Such studies have been done in many states, including New Jersey, Michigan, West Virginia, South Carolina, Oklahoma, New Mexico, and Tennessee, and in cities such as Tulsa, Boston, and Kalamazoo (Bartik 2013; Bartik, Gormley, and Adelstein 2012; Hustedt, Barnett, and Jung 2008; Hustedt et al. 2010; Weiland and Yoshikawa 2013; Wong et al. 2008).

These studies use a methodology called "regression discontinuity." This methodology relies on pre-K and kindergarten entrance being based on an age cutoff. Students entering pre-K, and students who graduated from pre-K and are entering kindergarten, are similar in family or program factors that led to pre-K participation. Selection bias should not be a big problem.

What does explain why one child is a pre-K entrant, and the other child is a pre-K graduate, is the child's age. The child entering kindergarten will on average be one year older than the child entering pre-K. But ages vary over a one-year period for each group. There are children entering pre-K who are just a few days younger than children entering kindergarten. These children should be similar in both observed and unobserved characteristics, except that the slightly older child has benefited from a year in a pre-K program.

We can estimate how much higher student test scores are at kindergarten entrance for those children who went to preschool, compared to children just starting in those same preschool programs. Using the variation in test scores with age, we can estimate how test scores vary with age. We can then see whether there is a "jump"—a "discontinuity"—in scores for the child who is just old enough for kindergarten entrance, and who has experienced a year of pre-K, versus the child who is a little too young for kindergarten entrance, and therefore is just entering pre-K.

Figure 2.1 shows an example of this jump in student test scores associated with Tulsa's pre-K program (Bartik, Gormley, and Adelstein 2012). The figure shows fall test scores along the vertical axis for groups of Tulsa students, sorted along the horizontal axis by age.[20] The students to the left of the vertical line are too young to enter kindergarten and are just entering Tulsa's pre-K program. The students to the right of the vertical line are former Tulsa pre-K participants who are just entering kindergarten. All these students were given the same tests at the same time in the fall.

Test scores in most of the figure go up smoothly with age. But there is an abrupt jump at the cutoff between pre-K entrants and kindergarten entrants. The most plausible explanation of this jump is that Tulsa's pre-K program increases test scores. The students just to the left and right of the cutoff are almost the same age, are shown in the full study to be similar in all observed characteristics, and differ mainly in that the group just to the right has had one year of Tulsa pre-K. Therefore, it seems likely that the jump is due to pre-K.[21]

Many studies have found such test score jumps in comparing entrants in state pre-K programs with kindergarten entrants who are pre-K graduates. These test score jumps tend to be in the range of increasing student learning during the pre-K year by perhaps 40 to 80 percent, compared to what children would learn on their own, without the state pre-K program.[22]

We can combine the estimated impact of state pre-K on kindergarten test scores, and the estimated impact of kindergarten scores on adult earnings, to predict how much these state pre-K programs increase adult earnings. These calculations suggest that state and local pre-K programs increase future adult earnings of children from low-income families by 6 to 15 percent.[23]

The study of Tulsa's full-day pre-K program by Bartik, Gormley, and Adelstein (2012) estimates test score effects that imply average adult earnings effects, for children from low-income families, of 10 percent. A study of Boston's full-day pre-K program by Weiland and Yoshikawa (2013) estimates test score effects that imply

Figure 2.1   How Test Scores of Tulsa Pre-K Entrants and Former Pre-K Students Vary with Age

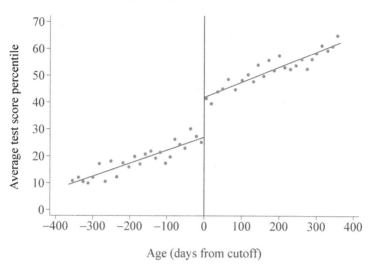

SOURCE: Bartik, Gormley, and Adelstein (2012).

average adult earnings effects, for children from low-income families, of 15 percent.[24]

SUMMARY OF THE EVIDENCE

We have better evidence for the effectiveness of early childhood education than for almost any social or educational intervention. We have better evidence because we have good comparison groups. Ironically, these good comparison groups arise because early childhood education is not universal, so many children are excluded from services.

Early childhood education has more evidence for effectiveness than most educational programs and practices. Consider the evidence for whether children benefit from going to third grade. No evidence from random assignment or natural experiments shows that children do any better from attending third grade rather than staying home. For third grade, we are unable to get good comparison groups, because everyone goes to third grade.

But how do these adult earnings benefits for high-quality early childhood education compare with program costs? The next chapter considers this important issue.

Timmy's been selected for the control group. He can't attend 3rd grade.

Chapter 3

How Do the Adult Earnings Benefits of High-Quality Early Childhood Education Compare to Costs?

As reviewed in Chapter 2, rigorous research shows that early childhood education can on average increase adult earnings for disadvantaged children by 3 to 26 percent. But are these earnings benefits greater than program costs?

FUTURE EARNINGS VERSUS PRESENT COSTS

To bring these ideas into focus, Figure 3.1 summarizes adult earnings benefits for three high-quality programs. The future adult earnings benefits reported for all three programs are for child participants from low-income families. A high-quality full-day pre-K program, similar to Tulsa's program, could increase average future adult earnings of such children by 10 percent.[25] A high-quality full-time, full-year child care and pre-K program from birth to age five, similar to the Abecedarian/Educare programs, could increase the average future adult earnings of low-income children by 26 percent. A high-quality home-visiting program to support parenting for children from low-income families, similar to the Nurse Family Partnership program, could increase the average future adult earnings of participant children by 3 percent.[26]

But costs must be considered. An Abecedarian/Educare program costs over $18,000 per year per child, or over $90,000 for the five years.[27] One year of high-quality full-day pre-K at age four costs around $10,000.[28] The Nurse Family Partnership costs $4,500 per

Figure 3.1 Average Percentage Increase in Adult Earnings for Three Early Childhood Education Programs

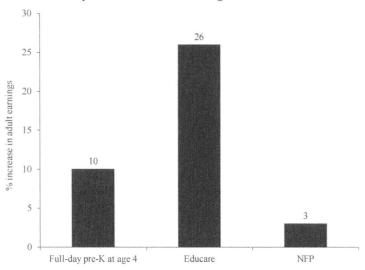

SOURCE: Author's calculations, based on sources described in text and endnotes.

child per year, or over $11,000 for the two-and-a-half years from the prenatal period until the child is age two.[29]

To compare benefits with costs, both must be expressed in today's dollars. The program costs are incurred today or in the next few years. The earnings benefits for former child participants are realized 15 to 60 years in the future. We first correct for inflation and express future earnings in terms of today's purchasing power. But even after that inflation correction, we must make a further correction, because a dollar today could be saved and invested and earn interest. Therefore, a dollar today will be worth much more than a dollar 50 years from now, because of interest compounding over time. Economists do these adjustments by discounting future dollars down in value, using an appropriate interest rate, so that future dollars are equivalent to today's dollars. This is referred to as calculating the "present value" of these future dollars. For example, even if there is no inflation, if we discount future dollars at 3 percent per year, one dollar received 50 years from now will have a "present value," in today's dollars, of only 23 cents.

Comparing the present value of earnings benefits to costs for these three programs, full-day pre-K at age four for low-income children has the highest ratio of adult earnings benefits to costs, at over 5-to-1. The program increases the present value of future earnings per child by an average of slightly over $50,000, at a cost of around $10,000. Five years of Abecedarian/Educare has earnings benefits of over $130,000 per child. But the program's costs are so high that the ratio of earnings benefits to costs is only 1.5-to-1. The Nurse Family Partnership is cheaper, but also has lower benefits for the child's future, resulting in a ratio of earnings benefits to costs of around 1.5-to-1. Table 3.1 summarizes these calculations.[30]

These ratios of earnings benefits to costs, ranging from 1.5-to-1 up to more than 5-to-1, are typical of high-quality early childhood programs. This implies that to achieve very large percentage earnings effects on future earnings, the programs must make significant investments per child. For example, for a child age four from a disadvantaged family, the present value of that child's future career earnings exceeds $500,000. A high-percentage increase in such a large number is a large benefit number in dollars, which will require large dollar costs if benefit-cost ratios do not typically exceed 6-to-1.

Table 3.1 Per-Child Earnings Benefits versus Costs of Three Early Childhood Programs

	Full-day pre-K at age four	Educare	NFP
Earnings benefits	$53,000	$134,000	$16,000
Program costs	$10,000	$87,000	$11,000
Ratio of benefits to costs	5.3	1.5	1.5

NOTE: Benefits and costs are rounded to nearest thousand, in present-value 2012 dollars. Present value is calculated at age four for pre-K, at birth for Educare/NFP. All benefits and costs are average effects per child participant.
SOURCE: Author's calculations based on research, as described in text and endnotes.

These calculations also imply that an early childhood program may pass a benefit-cost test even if its percentage effects on future earnings are modest. Even 2 percent of a half-million dollars in future earnings is a large benefit.

PARENTAL EARNINGS

In addition to earnings benefits for former child participants, some early childhood programs significantly boost the earnings of parents. Child care programs allow parents to work or go to school, which boosts earnings both in the short run and the long run. Some parenting programs, such as the Nurse Family Partnership, help change the life course of parents—for example, through encouraging job training, which may boost earnings.

For the Abecedarian program, parental earnings benefits have a present value of over 150 percent of the large earnings benefits for children. For the Nurse Family Partnership, parental earnings benefits have a present value that is equal to the present value of earnings benefits for children (Bartik 2011). For these two programs, including parental earnings roughly doubles the benefit-cost ratios in Table 3.1.

In contrast, just providing pre-K full-time during the school year at age four does not provide much of a direct earnings boost for parents.[31] Pre-K needs to cover more hours, a greater part of the year, and more years to significantly boost parental earnings prospects.

ARE THESE EFFECTS LARGE?

Early childhood education programs can increase adult earnings of child participants by 26 percent (Educare), 10 percent (full-day pre-K), or 3 percent (Nurse Family Partnership). A skeptic might admit that 26 percent is large, or even 10 percent, but is 3 percent really a large effect? The answer is "yes," for several reasons. First, most of us would welcome a 3 percent lifetime gain in our standard of living. Second, this percentage earnings effect is averaged over all program participants. Behind this average is a diversity of earnings gains for different individuals. Many have little or no gain from the program; others have much larger earnings gains.

How do we tell whether these large earnings gains for some former child participants are worth investing in the program? By comparing benefits with costs. These programs have a good economic payoff in that benefits significantly exceed costs. Early childhood programs do not solve all problems for all program participants. But early childhood programs do enough good for a sufficient number of child participants that they make economic sense. Added to these benefits for former child participants are social benefits for others, as discussed in Chapter 6.

CLOSING COMMENTS

These calculations of earnings-benefits-to-costs ratios assume that the research in Chapter 2 is valid. This research has been criticized, as is discussed in the next chapter.

Chapter 4

Criticisms of the Research Evidence

The research evidence for early childhood education has been questioned by critics, including the *Wall Street Journal* editorial page, Russ Whitehurst of the Brookings Institution, Charles Murray of the American Enterprise Institute, and Shikha Dalmia and Lisa Snell of the Reason Foundation. These criticisms have been repeated in news coverage by FactCheck.org and National Public Radio.

These critics raise the following issues:

- The evidence for early childhood education is argued to be based on small experiments conducted a long time ago by researchers; therefore, critics contend, we don't know whether early childhood education will work if run today at a large scale by ordinary public agencies.

- The recent Head Start experiment is argued to show that test score benefits of pre-K fade to statistical insignificance by third grade.

- Data from Oklahoma and Georgia are used to argue that universal pre-K fails to significantly improve test scores or other social indicators.

- A random assignment study of Tennessee's pre-K program is used to argue against the effectiveness of state and local pre-K programs.

These criticisms are overblown. As argued below, none of these criticisms successfully challenge the research consensus: High-quality early childhood education works.

CRITICISM 1: The evidence for early childhood education's benefits only comes from small and expensive experiments run a long time ago.

Critics acknowledge that evidence for early childhood education is provided by the Perry and Abecedarian experiments. But this evidence is argued to be irrelevant to policy today:[32]

> *Costs per participant for Perry and Abecedarian were multiples of the levels of investment in present-day state preschool programs.* (Whitehurst 2013b)[33]
>
> *[A] nationwide expansion of early education . . . won't have the highly motivated administrators and hand-picked staffs that demonstration projects enjoy.* (Murray 2013)[34]
>
> *The circumstances of the very poor families of the Black children who were served by these model programs 30 to 40 years ago are very different from those faced by the families that are presently served by publicly funded preschool programs. . . . [Forty] years ago other government supports for low-income families were at much lower levels and pre-K was not widely available for anyone.* (Whitehurst 2013b)[35]

However, the research evidence for early childhood education encompasses more than Perry and Abecedarian. Evidence comes from more recent studies of large-scale programs with more modest costs. As discussed in Chapter 2, many large-scale state and local pre-K programs have strong effects on short-run test scores; such effects predict sizable long-run earnings benefits. The Chicago Child-Parent Center studies provide direct evidence of long-run benefits. CPC was a large-scale program, with similar costs per child to many state and local pre-K programs.

More recent programs have smaller earnings benefits than Perry and Abecedarian. CPC has average earnings effects of 8 percent, and many state and local pre-K programs have effects from 6 to 10 percent, whereas Perry had earnings effects of 19 percent and Abecedarian had earnings effects of 26 percent. But because costs are lower, the benefit-cost ratio for recent pre-K programs is still strong. As Chapter 3 showed, a full-day pre-K program might have a ratio of earnings benefits to costs of over 5-to-1, whereas Abecedarian's high costs lead to a lower ratio of earnings benefits to costs of 1.5-to-1.

Today's pre-K programs are run at a large scale by state agencies and local public schools, not by expert researchers who handpick a few great teachers. For example, the public schools in Tulsa, Boston, and Chicago all run successful pre-K programs.

The presence of competing programs complicates benefit-cost analyses. If a new pre-K program substitutes for existing programs, this reduces the new program's net earnings benefits. But net costs of the new program are also reduced, because it reduces spending on existing programs. The ratio of benefits to costs need not decline.

Fewer of these recent evaluations are random assignment experiments. Random assignment experiments are expensive, and they are difficult to set up for a large-scale program. Such experiments will always be rare and will tend to be small-scale. But, as argued in Chapter 2, these recent evaluations are reliable because they have good comparison groups, chosen by natural experiments.

The recent studies look at test score effects in the short term, not directly at adult earnings effects. Benefits for adult earnings are inferred from test score effects. But this is inevitable if one wants timely evaluations of recent programs.

Finally, the Perry and Abecedarian evidence is still relevant to current policy issues. Today's Educare program is similar to Abecedarian. Today's pre-K programs have many similarities to Perry. Today's programs do have larger class sizes than Perry, and they usually only last one year rather than Perry's two years. On the other hand, Perry was a half-day program, whereas many current pre-K programs are full-day. All in all, Abecedarian and Perry are similar enough to today's programs to provide useful information for current policy.

CRITICISM 2: Early childhood education is argued to be ineffective because the recent Head Start experiment has test score effects that quickly faded to statistical insignificance.

Critics have argued that the recent random assignment experiment on Head Start trumps other research evidence and shows that large-scale early childhood education is ineffective:

The Head Start Impact Study is a randomized controlled trial, the gold-standard for evaluating the effectiveness of social and health programs. . . . The findings . . . are that there were effects favoring Head Start children on some outcome variables at the end of the Head Start year. However, these impacts did not persist. Both in the kindergarten and first grade follow-up data . . . , and the third grade follow-up data, . . . there were no reliable differences in outcomes for children who won the lottery to attend Head Start vs. those who lost that lottery and served as the control group. (Whitehurst 2013a)

Head Start's impact is no better than random. (*Wall Street Journal*, editorial published on February 27, 2013).[36]

These criticisms are based on the Head Start experiment's finding that estimated effects decline by third grade so that they are insignificantly different from zero. Based on literacy and math tests administered both at the end of Head Start and the end of third grade, the effects of Head Start decline by over 70 percent. The point estimate of test score effects at the end of third grade still predicts that Head Start will increase lifetime earnings by 1.2 percent, which is a lot of money over a career. But because of statistical uncertainty, we cannot reject that the true effect is zero or negative. The true effect could also be three times as great. However, if one begins with a skeptical attitude that the true effect is zero until proven otherwise, then the Head Start results at Grade Three do not overcome that skepticism.[37] If the Head Start random assignment experiment was the only evidence on the effects of early childhood education, skepticism about these programs' effectiveness would be warranted.

However, many early childhood programs have fading test score impacts, but still significantly improve adult outcomes. As shown in Chapter 2, test score fading occurs not only in Head Start, but in many early childhood programs, including Perry Preschool, the Abecedarian Project, and the Chicago Child-Parent Center Program. Despite this test score fading, adult earnings effects reemerge. The initial test score effects are better predictions of adult earnings effects than the faded test score effects. Figure 4.1 illustrates the evidence for these four programs (Head Start, Perry, Abecedarian, CPC).[38]

This fading and reemergence of effects could be due to non-cognitive skills, which are important to adult earnings but harder to measure using standardized tests. Social skills and character skills are at least as important as cognitive skills in making a worker more employable and more productive. Worker employability and productivity will depend upon social skills such as how a worker relates to supervisors, coworkers, and customers, and upon character skills such as reliability in showing up at work on time and being persistent in finishing work assignments. Cognitive skills also matter to adult earnings, but these cognitive skills must be applied effectively, which depends on character skills and social skills.

Figure 4.1   Predicted Percentage Effects on Adult Earnings of Early Childhood Programs, Based on Test Scores versus Adult Outcomes

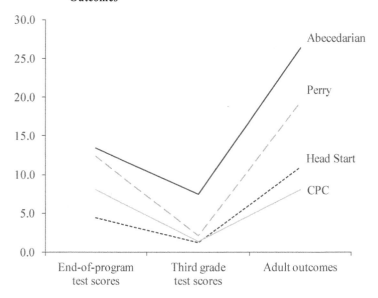

SOURCE: Author's calculations, based on research described in text and notes.

Pre-K can get children off to a good start by developing basic cognitive skills, social skills, and character skills. Over time, these skills build on themselves. If a child has better cognitive skills, social skills, and character skills at kindergarten entrance, that child will learn more in kindergarten and will develop still more self-confidence, ability to learn, and ability to operate socially in school. And so on in first grade and higher grades—at each grade, the skills built in previous grades lead to additional learning. By third grade, the boost to skills provided by pre-K is inadequately measured by standardized tests, as much of the boost comes from social and character skills that are harder to measure. But the initial boost to cognitive skills at kindergarten entrance is a catalyst that leads to these broader skills, by increasing self-confidence and the ability to learn. The important catalytic role of cognitive skills is why the end-of-program test score gain helps predict adult earnings.

Another important point is that the recent Head Start experiment may not represent the effectiveness of the best pre-K programs, Head Start in the past, or Head Start compared to no pre-K. Several studies show that initial test score effects of Head Start are one-half to two-thirds of some other pre-K programs.[39] Furthermore, the recent Head Start experiment's results are unusual in the rapidity of fade-out, compared both to other pre-K programs and to Head Start in the past. For example, Deming (2009) found little fading of Head Start's initial effects in elementary school, with more fading occurring in middle school.[40]

A possible explanation is that the Head Start experiment does not compare Head Start with no pre-K; it compares a treatment group offered enrollment in Head Start with a control group that was supposed to be denied admission to Head Start but often attended some pre-K program. Only 80 percent of the treatment group enrolled in Head Start. About half of the control group attended some pre-K program, including 14 percent in Head Start and 35 percent in some other pre-K program (Puma et al. 2012, p. xix; U.S. Department of Health and Human Services 2010). If these other pre-K programs were more effective than Head Start, the experiment's net impact would be reduced. In recent years, Head Start has faced more competition. Studies showing long-run benefits of Head Start are necessarily examining Head Start in the past, when low-income families had fewer high-quality alternatives. In recent years, increased availability of state pre-K means that Head Start needs to up its quality to justify its higher costs. But today's lower net Head Start impacts need not imply that high-quality pre-K makes no difference compared to no pre-K.

Recent Head Start reforms may have increased quality, compared to Head Start at the time of the experiment (2002–2003). From 2003 to 2006, more literacy instruction was pushed in Head Start. Research suggests that Head Start children gained more in literacy in 2006 and 2009 than was true in 2003 (Barnett 2013).

CRITICISM 3: Why haven't Oklahoma and Georgia, two states that have prominently adopted universal pre-K, been more obviously successful in improving test scores and other social indicators?

Pre-K advocates have sometimes pointed to Oklahoma and Georgia as models (Lerner 2012; Obama 2013). These states were early adopters of broader pre-K access (Georgia in 1995, Oklahoma in 1998), and have moved a long way toward universal access. (Oklahoma has 74 percent of all four-year-olds in its state program; Georgia has 58 percent [Barnett et al. 2013].) Oklahoma's program meets high-quality standards (Barnett et al.) and has received favorable evaluations (Wong et al. 2008). (Georgia's pre-K program has more mixed reviews.)

But, critics argue, if broad access to pre-K is so great, why haven't Oklahoma and Georgia made more progress? Shikha Dalmia and Lisa Snell of the Reason Foundation hold that "neither state program has demonstrated major social benefits. . . . The average NAEP reading score for Oklahoma fourth-graders dropped four points between 1998 and 2011—although it went up nine points for Georgia. . . . Oklahoma remains below the national average and Georgia has just reached the national average" (Dalmia and Snell 2013).

The *Wall Street Journal* editorial board quotes President Obama, from a Georgia speech promoting federal support for preschool, as saying that "education has to start at the earliest possible age. . . . If you are looking for a good bang for your educational buck, this is it right here." The *Journal* goes on to assert that "Mr. Obama is right that the state is a good example of what universal pre-K can buy. Georgia's fourth- and eighth-grade reading, math and science scores all trail the national average" (*Wall Street Journal* 2013).

Both pre-K critics and advocates need to recognize that analysis of test scores in just one or two states is subject to great uncertainty. Because average state test scores are frequently buffeted by demographic or economic changes, detecting the influence of any policy on test scores in one or two states is statistically difficult. Even if a state's pre-K program improves test scores enough to predict large long-term benefits, these improvements can easily be masked by other influences.

Part of the empirical challenge is that even slight improvements in test scores are sufficient to predict large economic gains. A two percentile gain in average elementary school test scores—moving from the 50th to the 52nd percentile on a standardized test—is enough to predict that future adult earnings will increase by 1 percent (Chetty et al. 2011). For the average American worker, career earnings exceed $1.5 million.[41] A 1 percent boost would increase career earnings by over $15,000, a large benefit. Demographic and economic changes can easily affect test scores by more than two percentiles. Because of this statistical "noise" in a state's average test scores, it is hard for an examination of one state's test scores to rule out test score increases that would be meaningful economically.[42]

A good recent study of pre-K in Oklahoma and Georgia tries to minimize this uncertainty by combining many years of data (Cascio and Schanzenbach 2013). This study estimates average state test score effects that predict that benefits exceed costs by at least 3-to-1.[43] However, because of the statistical noise inherent in focusing on test score effects in just two states, these estimated test score effects are not statistically significantly different from zero at conventional levels of significance used by researchers.[44]

People love anecdotes. We are tempted to believe that the truth can be discovered by the examples of one or two states. But this is difficult to do. If states are laboratories of democracy, this lab gets much more precise results with many "test subjects" (states), rather than with just one or two states as test subjects. An alternative way to get the larger numbers needed for statistical precision is to compare many individuals, some of whom participated in early childhood education versus similar nonparticipants.

CRITICISM 4: The recent Tennessee pre-K experiment shows that test score effects quickly fade, which raises questions about whether state pre-K programs are effective.

A recent random-assignment experimental study of Tennessee's pre-K program found some effects at the end of pre-K, but effects faded by the end of kindergarten or the end of first grade (Lipsey et al. 2013a,b). According to one critic,

> *I see these findings as devastating for advocates of the expansion of state pre-K programs. This is the first large scale randomized trial of a present-day state pre-K program. Its methodology soundly trumps the quasi-experimental approaches that have heretofore been the only source of data on which to infer the impact of these programs. . . . The most defensible conclusion is that these statewide programs are not working to meaningfully increase the academic achievement or social/emotional skills and dispositions of children from low-income families.*
> (Whitehurst 2013c)

One problem with the Tennessee study is its considerable sample attrition, which may lead to bias. In the first cohort of children, the

Tennessee study only obtained parental consent to have tests administered to the children for 46 percent of the pre-K participants and for 32 percent of the control group. For the sample with test data, the treatment and control groups may differ greatly in unobserved characteristics, particularly since the attrition differs so much in the two groups. Any test score differences between the two groups will be due to some combination of true effects of the pre-K program and bias due to unobserved characteristics. The Tennessee researchers do a good job of minimizing biases by controlling for the child's and family's observed characteristics. But such controls cannot adjust for biases due to unobserved characteristics.[45]

Because of these problems, the Tennessee study does not trump other studies of state and local pre-K programs. As discussed in Chapter 2, these other studies try to estimate effects of pre-K by natural experiments in which pre-K access varies because of where a family lives or a child's age. The argument is that such natural variation in pre-K access will cause the treatment and comparison groups to be similar in unobserved characteristics. While a random assignment study with few problems may be superior to natural experiments, a random assignment study with sizable attrition cannot claim such superiority.

Another important point is that Tennessee's pre-K program is not as high-quality as other state and local pre-K programs. For example, Tennessee spends a little under $6,000 per child annually for a full-day pre-K program. According to Barnett et al. (2013), Tennessee would have to spend at least $2,000 extra per child to consistently deliver quality.[46] In contrast, pre-K programs such as those in Tulsa, Chicago, and Boston all pay amounts per child that equal or exceed guidelines for the funding necessary to reach quality standards. Even if Tennessee's program is ineffective, this need not imply the ineffectiveness of state and local pre-K programs of better quality.

One study of one state's program rarely trumps all other studies. Any single study has limitations, which is why policy should be based on many studies. The case for early childhood education is that high-quality programs work, not that all programs work.

CONCLUDING COMMENTS

A persistent theme in these criticisms is that the effectiveness of early childhood education is uncertain. Uncertainty argues for postponing action until we know more. Russ Whitehurst of Brookings makes precisely this argument in discussing the Tennessee results: "Maybe we should figure out how to deliver effective programs before the federal government funds preschool for all" (Whitehurst 2013c). But, as this book will discuss in Chapter 5, we do know something about how to deliver effective programs.

Chapter 5

How Can Early Childhood Education Programs Best Be Designed?

Early childhood programs can have benefits that exceed costs. But how does this benefit-cost ratio vary with program design, such as

- quality of teacher-child interactions;
- class size and teacher credentials and salaries;
- whether the program serves only low-income children, or also serves middle-class children;
- program duration (two years versus one year of pre-K; full-day versus half-day pre-K); and
- earlier versus later interventions—for example, programs at ages one and two versus at ages three and four.

QUALITY OF TEACHER-CHILD INTERACTIONS

An unsurprising research finding is that the effectiveness of early childhood education depends on the quality of teacher-child interactions. If teacher-child interactions are better, children make more progress in early childhood programs (Mashburn et al. 2008; Sabol et al. 2013).[47]

Better-quality teacher-child interactions include better instructional support—for example, the teacher posing thought-provoking questions to children and providing meaningful feedback. Better-quality interactions also include good classroom management and positive emotional support. The quality of teacher-child interactions can be measured using trained observers who rate what is going on in a pre-K classroom at various times during the day (LaParo, Pianta, and Stuhlman 2004). Better-quality teacher-child interactions are correlated with learning gains that are meaningful economically. One study divided pre-K classrooms into four levels of quality based on teacher-child interactions. The differences in test-score gains between the highest-quality and lowest-quality classrooms predict future earnings differences of 6 percent.[48]

Such adult earnings gains sum to large earnings benefits for an entire classroom. Suppose we consider a pre-K classroom that has 15 children, all from disadvantaged families. Then, a 6 percent average boost to adult earnings for 15 children would have a present value of slightly less than one-half million dollars.[49] If we could sustain this classroom improvement, then each year would yield another half-million dollars in increased future earnings.

This comparison is for improving pre-K classrooms from the lowest- to the highest-quality level. Evidence suggests that quality improvements have increasing effects at higher-quality levels. But even more modest-quality increases can have benefits per classroom cohort of over $100,000.[50]

Large costs are justified to improve the average quality of early childhood education by a moderate amount. When multiplied by an entire future for a child, and many children in each classroom, and potentially many years if the program can sustain the higher quality, even modest improvements in average quality have large payoffs.

CLASS SIZE AND TEACHER CREDENTIALS

A more controversial issue among researchers is how early childhood education's effectiveness is altered by "structural quality." "Structural quality" means program features such as class size and teacher credentials and salaries. These features of the program's "structure" can easily be set by program rules and funding.

Structural quality makes a difference in some studies, but not in others.[51] Structural quality is not assigned randomly or by natural experiment, so these studies may be biased by unobserved child and family characteristics. In contrast, a random assignment experiment shows that the Nurse Family Partnership yields better outcomes if services are provided by nurses, rather than paraprofessionals (Olds et al. 2004).

Despite this mixed research, it seems prudent for policymakers to assume that smaller class sizes and stronger teacher credentials will facilitate greater program effectiveness. One rationale for this policy advice is that it seems plausible: Better teacher-child interactions are probably easier to attain if the class size is more modest and the teacher is better trained.

Second, some of the best pre-K programs with favorable evaluations used certified teachers and had moderate class sizes. This is true for Perry, Abecedarian, Chicago CPC, and some good local pre-K programs, including Tulsa and Boston.[52] Lowering quality standards too much from these models increases the risk of lower effectiveness.

Third, only modest increases in effectiveness are needed for smaller class sizes and stronger teacher credentials to have future earnings benefits that exceed costs. Suppose for a pre-K program we increased the lead teacher credential requirement from only requiring a Child Development Associate (CDA) credential to requiring a certified teacher with a BA who is paid a public school wage. For a class size of 15 children and two teachers, this increased credential requirement increases the cost per child of a full-day (six-hour) school-year pre-K program by about one-third, from around $7,500 to around $10,000. But these increased costs would be justified by higher earnings benefits if such a change only increased average future adult earnings by one-half of 1 percent. Only a small percentage earnings increase is needed, because expected future career earnings are so large, even for disadvantaged children, averaging over one-half million dollars in present value. This earnings increase would be predicted to occur if average end-of-program test scores increased by two-thirds of one percentile—for example, moving a student from the median (50th percentile) to the 50.67th percentile (test scores greater than 50.67 percent of all students).[53]

Lowering class size in a full-day pre-K program from 20 students to 15 students would increase the costs per child from $8,300 to $10,000. This would have earnings benefits greater than costs if it increased adult earnings by only 0.3 percent. This would be predicted to occur if end-of-program test scores increased by one-half of one percentile.[54]

Suppose that lowering class size in pre-K was as effective in raising test scores as it is in grades K–3. Suppose also that we base this extrapolation to pre-K on a random assignment experiment, the Tennessee Class Size Study, which looked at lowering class size in kindergarten through third grade. If the Tennessee results are extrapolated to pre-K, lowering pre-K class size from 20 to 15 children would increase future adult earnings by 30 percent.[55]

The mixed research findings on class size and teacher credentials may be due to how these policies interact with other quality determinants. Mandating lower pre-K class sizes may make it more difficult to afford adequate teacher salaries. Lower salaries will increase teacher turnover, which may hurt pre-K quality. Higher teacher credential requirements without increases in pre-K teacher wages may also increase teacher turnover. Policymakers need to consider how the combined features of program design affect quality.

MIDDLE-CLASS CHILDREN

Research suggests that middle-class children's benefits from early childhood education vary by program type. For pre-K, benefits occur for a wide variety of income groups. For child care and parenting programs, benefits are limited to children from low-income families.

Across children from families with different income, pre-K has similar effects on improving a child's test score percentile at kindergarten entrance. In both Tulsa's and Boston's universal pre-K pro-grams, children eligible for a lunch subsidy have greater test-score percentile gains than children whose family income is too high for a lunch subsidy, but the advantage is slight and usually statistically insignificant.[56]

Increases in kindergarten test scores by a given percentile pre-dict a similar dollar gain in adult earnings (Chetty et al. 2011). Say test scores increase by one percentile. Whether that one percentile is gained from the 20th to the 21st percentile or from the 70th to the 71st percentile doesn't matter—in either case, it would result in a very similar amount of dollars being added to future adult annual earnings. Therefore, Tulsa or Boston pre-K participants from different income groups would be predicted to have similar future dollar gains in adult earnings.

Why are earnings effects of pre-K similar across income groups? Quality pre-K provides services that are difficult for even the best par-ent with the most resources to reproduce on his or her own. Quality pre-K provides opportunities to learn to get along with peers and with authority figures such as teachers. Quality pre-K provides peer pres-sure and teacher help in learning cognitive skills. This child-centered learning is hard for most parents to provide completely with their own resources.

Some parents may have sufficient resources to purchase quality pre-K on their own. But quality pre-K is expensive—costing, as men-tioned, $10,000 for a full-day (six hours per day) school-year pro-gram. Costs are even higher if we add in wraparound hours for the rest of the workday, and for the rest of the year, or if we consider adding in a second year of pre-K.

Such expensive services are difficult for most families to afford on their own. Many middle-class as well as low-income families will find it challenging to pay for quality pre-K on their own dime.

A high proportion of American children under the age of five live in families with modest resources. Based on data from the Cur-rent Population Survey, of children under the age of five, about one-quarter are in families below the poverty line, and almost half (47 percent) are below 200 percent of the poverty line. Even if pre-K was needed only for children from poor and near-poor families, full-scale pre-K would need to serve half of all American children. But many children from families above 200 percent of the poverty line will also benefit from public funding for quality pre-K. These working-class and middle-class families find that publicly funded pre-K can provide an educational opportunity for their child that the family could not readily match.

Even though high-quality pre-K provides similar dollar benefits to children from low-income and middle-class families, universal pre-K would still help even out economic opportunities. Expected baseline future earnings—earnings without pre-K—would be much lower for the average child from a lower-income family, compared to one from a middle-income family. Similar dollar benefits for children from lower-income and middle-income families imply much larger percentage effects on future earnings prospects for children from lower-income families.

Table 5.1 shows a simulation of how pre-K benefits vary across income groups.[57] Even though pre-K's dollar benefits for future adult earnings of middle-class children are nine-tenths of the dollar benefits for lower-income children, the percentage boost to earnings for lower-income children is twice that for middle-class children (10 percent versus 5 percent).

In contrast, effects of developmental child care programs or parenting programs appear to be limited to low-income families. Consider the Infant Health and Development Program mentioned in Chapter 2. IHDP provided child care services for children at ages one and two that were similar to the Abecedarian/Educare programs. Duncan and Sojourner (2013) find large and statistically significant effects of this program on children whose family income was below 180 percent of the poverty line, but not for children from families above that income level.

Table 5.1 How Earnings Benefits of Pre-K per Child Vary for Children from Different Income Groups

	Earnings gains versus baseline earnings for a child from a	
	Low-income family	Middle-income family
Gains from pre-K	$53,000	$48,000
Baseline earnings	$547,000	$997,000
Percentage gain	10%	5%

NOTE: Gains and baseline earnings are rounded to the nearest thousand, in present-value 2012 dollars. Baseline earnings are the present value of total career earnings without pre-K. Earnings and gains are averages per child for program participants.
SOURCE: Author's calculations, as described in text and endnotes.

Effects of high-quality child care might be income-targeted because there are big differences across different-income families in what the high-quality child care is substituting for. The high-quality child care for lower-income families may be substituting for either parental or relative care by parents and relatives who may be over-stressed by poverty. Alternatively, the high-quality child care may be substituting for the very-low-quality child care the family can afford on its own. For middle-income families, even high-quality child care is substituting for parental or relative care by families that have fewer stressors and more resources, or for better-quality child care that a middle-income family can afford on its own. It is more difficult for a high-quality child care program to surpass what a middle-class family can provide on its own in child care at ages one and two.

Similar findings occur for parenting programs. For the Nurse Family Partnership, the research suggests that this program had greater effects for more disadvantaged women (Olds et al. 1997).

On average, middle-income families may have more resources and support to provide high-quality parenting on their own. On average, low-income families may be more likely to have fewer social supports and resources. Parenting programs might provide a valuable supplement.

PROGRAM DURATION

There are some signs of diminishing returns to duration for pre-K programs. A full-day pre-K program seems to have effects that are one-half to two-thirds greater than a half-day program, rather than the doubled effects one might expect. In Tulsa, half-day pre-K is predicted to increase future earnings of the children with the lowest income by 6 percent, whereas a full-day program yields an increase of 10 percent for the same income group.[58]

Two years of pre-K does not double benefits. The estimates from the Chicago Child-Parent Center Program suggest that children who participated for two years, at both ages three and four, gained about 50 percent more in earnings than children who participated only at age four.[59]

Diminishing returns may occur for several reasons. First, pre-K for some children is making up for major skill deficiencies. Once a major skill deficiency is addressed sufficiently, it cannot be overcome again. Second, many children may only be able to learn a certain amount per day. Third, adding a second year may have diminishing returns if the pre-K curriculum cannot assume that all participants at age four have already participated at age three.

Despite these diminishing returns, moving from a half day to a full day, or from one year of pre-K to two years, probably passes a benefit-cost test. If one year of pre-K has future earnings benefits that are five times the costs, as shown in Chapter 3, then even earnings benefits of half as much for a second year will still be double the additional costs. For half-day versus full-day pre-K, similar simulations suggest added earnings benefits of four times the added costs for full-day.[60]

For full-day versus half-day pre-K, a full-day program makes it easier and more attractive for many parents to access the program. It is cheaper for parents to add on wraparound child care to turn a full-day pre-K program into a full child-care program. Added access increases benefits.

EARLIER VERSUS LATER INTERVENTIONS

How about returns to early childhood education programs at different ages? On average, many pre-K programs appear to have benefits for children's future earnings, compared to costs, that are greater than earnings-benefits-to-cost ratios for earlier-age child care or parenting programs.

This was apparent in Chapter 3, which found an earnings-benefits-to-costs ratio for full-day pre-K of over 5-to-1, versus earnings-benefits-to-costs ratios of 1.5-to-1 for Abecedarian/Educare and the Nurse Family Partnership. Similar findings were reported in a research review by Reynolds, Temple, and Ou (2010): "Although programs at all ages show evidence of positive economic returns exceeding $1 per dollar invested, preschool programs for three- and four-year-olds generally show the highest returns" (p. 181).[61]

For child care programs, the issue is high program costs per child. Abecedarian/Educare is predicted to increase the child's future earnings by 26 percent. But five years of full-time child care from six weeks after birth to age five has gross costs of $18,000 per year, or $90,000 in total.

A child care program has a hard time being as cost-efficient as a pre-K program. Child care programs have to operate with low ratios of children to caregivers to be high-quality. Pre-K programs can be high-quality with child-to-teacher ratios of 15-to-2, 17-to-2, or even 20-to-2, which obviously are infeasible for quality child care at ages one and two.

For parenting programs, the problem is that a good parenting program costs as much per child as a good pre-K program, but directly involves the child for fewer hours. A good parenting program requires frequent individual home visits. For example, the NFP includes around 30 individual home visits over two-and-a-half years at 90 minutes per visit. The total amount of time is about 45 hours of one-on-one attention. The idea of the program is that these individual home visits will transform parenting practices. And these programs work: The NFP increases the child's future earnings by around 3 percent on average.

In contrast, even a half-day, one-school-year pre-K program will involve the child directly for about 500 hours (three hours per day times 180 school days = 540 hours). A full-day program would be over 1,000 hours.

But the Nurse Family Partnership costs about $11,000 per child over that two-and-a-half-year period. Even a full-day pre-K program only costs about $10,000 per child. The reason for the cost differential is that the NFP requires so much one-on-one time with each individual parent by a skilled professional nurse. Pre-K serves children in groups, which from a cost perspective is more efficient.

A child's brain may be more malleable at ages zero, one, and two than at ages three and four. But the interventions at earlier ages have to be more one-on-one or in very small groups, which is expensive. In addition, these interventions substitute for what parents do on their own at these ages, which in many cases will be more than adequate. In contrast, pre-K interventions at ages three and four can be done successfully in larger groups, and they provide learning in social skills that children are ready for and can more easily get in a pre-K setting than on their own.

Pre-K services at ages three and four target an age range that is a "sweet spot": the child's brain is still malleable enough for modest interventions to have large long-run effects, but the child is old enough that the child is ready to learn in larger groups that are cost-effective to run. From a benefit-cost perspective, ages three and four offer the largest returns for a child's development per dollar spent.

Having said that, if we're trying to maximize our effects on each child's development, there are benefits to adding developmental child care and parenting programs for low-income children to the program mix. Pre-K is unlikely to increase lower-income children's future earnings by 26 percent, which an Abecedarian/Educare program can do. Parenting programs can add additional future earnings effects of 3 percent or more. These benefits to children's future earnings exceed the added costs of these program additions. And these program additions have benefits for parents that also should be considered.

A sensible proposal would be universal pre-K, along with income-targeted parenting programs and developmental child care. Such a proposal is described in Chapter 7.

First, however, I broaden the perspective on benefits. So far, the analysis has focused on the benefits of early childhood education for former child participants and their families. But are there broader social benefits? Chapter 6 considers this question.

He's only just started, but the spillover has really been pretty good.

Chapter 6

Spillover Benefits

How Does Early Childhood Education Affect Other Groups Than Those Families Directly Served by These Programs?

So far, this book has focused on how early childhood education benefits child participants or their parents. But what about the rest of society?

If I think my children will be OK without government intervention in early childhood education, why should I be willing to pay increased taxes for early childhood education to help "other people's children"? Altruism is one reason, but is there also an argument to be made based on enlightened self-interest?

Yes, there is: When some children get more skills, this has large spillover benefits for the rest of society. The most important spillover benefits, in my view, are the productivity benefits for the entire economy. Other spillover benefits include peer effects in education, lower crime, short-term and long-term fiscal benefits, and long-term benefits for the next generation.

SKILL SPILLOVERS

Some people picture the economy as having a fixed number of good jobs. If my children don't need government help for early childhood education, then I might think that expanding early childhood education harms my children's prospects.[62] It's more competition for the fixed number of good jobs.

But that's not how the economy works. The empirical evidence suggests that when skills of one group increase, this enhances overall wages of most workers. The underlying reason is that the number of good jobs is not fixed. Good jobs will expand in response to the supply of persons with good skills.

For example, studies by Ernesto Moretti and others have shown sizable positive effects of an increase in the college graduation percentage in a metro economy on the metro area's wages (Diamond 2013; Moretti 2003, 2004, 2012). My wages depend not only on whether I have a college degree, but also on what percentage of others in the local economy have a college degree.

Suppose we use these results to project the wage effects if a metro area has a 1 percent increase in the percentage of workers with a college degree. As shown in Figure 6.1, the direct effect on metro-area average wages would be an increase of 0.8 percent. College graduates on average earn 80 percent more than non–college graduates. Multiplying 80 percent by 1 percent yields a 0.8 percent increase in average wages.

But the estimated spillover effects of the college graduation percentage on others' wages imply that average wages for others in the economy will go up by 1.1 percent. The total wage increase will be 1.9 percent. The sum of the spillover effects is actually larger than the direct wage effect of increasing college graduates.

For any individual, the spillover effect is small. If I get a college degree, my expected earnings go up by 80 percent, which will add about $1.2 million to my income over an entire career.[63] The impact of this on any one individual fellow metro resident is small. But the spillover impact summed over the many other workers in the metro area is $1.7 million, slightly more than the direct effect on my earnings.[64]

Most workers in a local economy benefit from other workers having better skills. Even if my children would have great skills without early childhood education, their wages would still benefit from other people's children having more skills.

One reason for skill spillovers is that employers have to make decisions about technology use and job creation based on the overall supply of workers and skills, not on whether any given individual has skills. Even if I have great skills, if my coworkers have lousy skills,

Figure 6.1 Effects of a 1 Percent Increase in Metro Workers Who Are College Graduates on a Metro Area's Average Wages

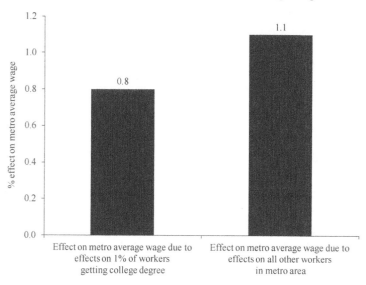

SOURCE:Author's calculations, based on studies by Moretti, as described in text.

my employer is going to have more trouble introducing new technologies. This will harm the competitiveness of my employer, which will damage my wages.

Even if all the workers at my firm have good skills, the firm will benefit if it can rely on quality products at good prices from local suppliers. This depends upon these local suppliers having a ready supply of skilled workers.

Finally, there are many industries that rely on obtaining ideas and workers from other firms in the same industry. This is part of the productivity advantage of local high-tech economies in Silicon Valley. The productivity of a firm may depend on the skills of workers in other competing firms, which provide a source of ideas for my firm.

The spillovers from competing firms and local suppliers have long been discussed in regional economics. They are called "agglomeration economies" and are characterized by productivity advantages from a cluster of an industry in a local economy. These agglomeration economies depend in part on worker skills.

This book's calculations in prior chapters of earnings gains for former child participants do not rely on spillover benefits.[65] With spillover benefits, the aggregate economic gain from early childhood education might be at least double what was previously stated.

How are these broad worker benefits realized? Employers will decide to expand, locate, or start up in a metro area because of the increased supply of workers with better skills. These employer decisions lead to more jobs and better jobs, and this benefits all the area's workers.

Realizing such benefits at the local level requires that a significant proportion of children remain in the same local economy in which they participated in early childhood education. The evidence indicates that this occurs. At least half of all Americans spend most of their career in the metropolitan area in which they spent their early childhood (Bartik 2011). Those who leave spread the productivity benefits of better skills to the broader state economy or to the national economy. Those who stay provide sizable spillover benefits for the local economy.[66]

PEER EFFECTS IN EDUCATION

These spillover wage effects provide a long-term argument for why I might want to pay higher taxes to help other people's children. Are there short-term arguments? One short-term argument is peer effects in education.

We know that there are peer effects in K–12 education. All children in a classroom tend to learn more during a given year if the average skill level in the classroom at the year's start is higher.

The magnitude of these estimated peer effects is sizable, at least 15 percent per school year (Hanushek et al. 2003; Hoxby 2000). If starting average achievement levels in a class are one grade level higher, then students in that class would be expected to learn about 0.15 grade levels more that year.

Some research provides direct evidence that pre-K provides peer benefits in K–12. Neidell and Waldfogel (2010) estimate models of kindergarten achievement that control for the percentage of peers enrolled in pre-K. They find that for every additional child who was enrolled in pre-K, the overall increase in test scores in the kindergarten class is from 16 to 50 percent higher than would be predicted based on the individual effect on that child.

If more children have higher skills, then teachers can spend more class time teaching to a higher standard. In addition, the teacher will need to spend less time bringing some individual children up to grade level. This frees up time for working individually with more students to match their learning needs. Also, if children enter the class with better behavior, classroom disruptions will be fewer, which will increase learning for all students.

Therefore, even if I already have the money to enroll my child in high-quality pre-K, or even if I think my child does not need high-quality pre-K, I have an interest in paying higher taxes for pre-K for other people's children, because it will enhance my child's learning in K–12.

SPILLOVERS FROM REDUCING CRIME

In addition to spillovers on the legal labor market, early childhood education reduces crime. When we enhance an individual's legal earnings prospects, we reduce the probability that that individual will become involved in criminal activity. Therefore, one other argument for why I should invest in other people's children is that it reduces my own and my children's probability of being a crime victim. This can be a powerful political argument. Furthermore, some evidence suggests that educational investments may be a more cost-effective way of fighting crime than longer prison sentences (Greenwood et al. 1998).

GOVERNMENT/TAXPAYER BENEFITS

Another spillover benefit of early childhood education is fiscal benefits. By "fiscal benefits" we mean either greater tax revenues at unchanged tax rates or less need for government spending. Such fiscal benefits allow governments to help taxpayers, either by lowering tax rates without cutting services, or by improving services without tax rate increases.

In the long run, the increased earnings due to early childhood education will be taxed by federal, state, and local governments. The increased earnings from early childhood education will also lower welfare usage, reducing the need for government spending. The drop in criminal activity will reduce prison costs and criminal justice system spending.

In the short run, early childhood education may reduce remedial education costs. Several studies suggest that early childhood education reduces special education costs. Special education costs can be an extra $10,000 per year per child. Most studies suggest some reduction in special education costs from early childhood education, although the magnitude varies widely, from 23 to 86 percent.[67]

Simulation studies conclude that in the long run, many early childhood education investments are self-financing. Estimates by Lynch (2007) suggest that after 43 years, high-quality universal pre-K's fiscal benefits will be about eight times program costs. Universal pre-K is estimated to break even from a combined federal and state government perspective after nine years, and for the average state after 23 years.

Other simulation estimates are more conservative, but they agree that in the long run, fiscal benefits exceed direct budget costs. Dickens and Baschnagel (2008) conclude that a universal version of the Perry Preschool Program, a relatively expensive program, would break even in budget terms after 49 years.

The problem is that policymakers must make decisions in the short run. And in the short run, early childhood education has fiscal costs. The long-run fiscal benefits accrue to a variety of government revenue and spending accounts, many outside the education system. The fiscal benefits are removed both in time and governmental function from the immediate fiscal costs of pre-K for an education budget.

PRE-K: THE NEXT GENERATION

Early childhood education may have important spillover benefits for the next generation. We know that parents' income has large effects on their child's future outcomes, especially for children in low-income families. Parent income in early childhood is particularly important.

Duncan, Ziol-Guest, and Kalil (2010) find that added parental income makes a bigger difference for a child's future adult earnings for children from low-income families. Duncan, Morris, and Rodrigues (2011) find that antipoverty experiments that boost family income appear to boost a child's academic performance.

Of particular interest is the finding that a child's future adult earnings are more affected by the income of the child's parents when the child is ages zero to five than by income in later childhood years. Once one controls for family income in early childhood, the family's income when the child is ages 6 through 15 has little impact on the child's future adult earnings.

Children at ages five or less are particularly vulnerable to stresses. Poverty produces numerous stresses, such as a family being forced to move, or a parent losing a job.

This raises the possibility that early childhood programs have next-generation benefits. If we invest now in early childhood education, then that raises the earnings of former childhood participants as adults. When these former participants form their own families, their family's income will be higher. This will lead to better childhood development in the next generation, and better adult outcomes for that generation. This virtuous cycle obviously can continue.

CONCLUDING COMMENTS

There are very large economic spillovers from investing in high-quality early childhood education programs. More speculative projections suggest that these economic spillovers extend into subsequent generations and make these programs self-financing in the long run.

But perhaps of more immediate interest, there are huge skill spillovers on most workers' wages from increasing overall skills. In a modern economy, workers are interdependent. We're in this economy together.

Chapter 7

A Proposed Early Childhood Education Strategy

Based on research, what early childhood education strategy would provide the greatest economic benefits? This chapter proposes three programs, suggests methods for quality control, and considers possible roles of the federal government versus state and local governments.

The proposed programs are

1. Universal full-day pre-K available to all four-year-olds, with teachers paid public school wages and with relatively small class sizes of around 15 children for 2 teachers;

2. Targeted full-time, full-year child care and pre-K available for all disadvantaged children from birth to age five, modeled after the Abecedarian and Educare programs;

3. Targeted parenting services for first-time disadvantaged mothers and their children from the prenatal period until age two, modeled after the Nurse Family Partnership.

FULL-DAY UNIVERSAL PRE-K FOR FOUR-YEAR-OLDS

Considering the pre-K proposal first, why this design? First, universal access, regardless of family income, would maximize aggregate economic impact. As discussed in Chapter 5, the available research evidence suggests that providing pre-K at age four to children from middle-class families has a high ratio of future earnings benefits to costs. If universal pre-K's benefits in future earnings are similar in dollar terms for most of the income distribution, then the aggregate economic impact of pre-K increases roughly proportionately with the number of children enrolled, and is greatest with universal access. A universal program would still be significantly redistributional, as the future earnings benefits would be a much greater percentage boost for children from lower-income families.

Furthermore, the broader the pre-K access, the greater the spill-over benefits in increasing the economy's productivity and most workers' wages (see Chapter 6). Higher skills for children from both lower-income and middle-income backgrounds would spill over to benefit the other group.

Universal access to pre-K might also provide positive peer effects in pre-K classrooms, increasing pre-K's effectiveness for lower-income children. Research suggests pre-K children benefit from having peers with higher skills. The spillover is 20 percent: Including more kids with higher test scores increases the class test scores by 20 percent more than predicted based on the direct effect (Henry and Rickman 2007).[68] No one thinks that the ideal pre-K design is income-segregated "separate but equal" programs. Yet this is what we do when we have Head Start limited to poor children, state programs targeting the near-poor, and private pre-K programs serving the upper class.

Universal access pre-K is likely to have broader political popularity. However, the primary rationale for universal access is not political expediency, but larger economic benefits.

A full-day pre-K program is likely more attractive to many families, because it minimizes child care costs and hassles of arranging wraparound child care. This easier access will increase program take-up rates and thereby aggregate economic impact. A full-day program does have somewhat lower bang for the buck than a half-day program. But the incremental benefits of full-day programs over half-day programs exceed costs even if take-up rates do not increase. The higher take-up rate adds additional economic benefits.

The universal program would be restricted to age four because there is no research on the benefits of age three pre-K for middle-class children. As discussed below, age three pre-K for disadvantaged children would be provided by a targeted program.

The pre-K program would lean toward being overfunded for high quality, by paying public school wages and having low class sizes. As discussed in Chapter 5, the research on these "structural" quality features is inconclusive. But it is prudent to imitate the pre-K programs with the greatest success, such as Perry, Chicago CPC, Tulsa, and Boston, which pay high salaries and have modest class sizes.

TARGETED EDUCARE/ABECEDARIAN FOR ALL DISADVANTAGED CHILDREN

In addition to universal pre-K, the proposal includes an Educare/ Abecedarian program offering free education-oriented child care and pre-K full-time from six weeks of age up to age five to the neediest children. The income targeting of this program is justified by the research that suggests that such comprehensive child care provides significant benefits only for children from lower-income backgrounds. The Educare/Abecedarian model would be used because it has the most extensive research evidence.

The 26 percent adult earnings boost from Educare/Abecedarian is over two-and-a-half times the 10 percent earnings boost that disadvantaged children might get from full-day pre-K. Table 7.1 shows that adding on Educare to full-day pre-K for disadvantaged children has added earnings benefits that exceed the added costs. The benefit-cost ratio for this addition is only slightly above one, but the dollar

Table 7.1 Benefits versus Costs per Child of Adding Educare to Pre-K

	Full-day pre-K at age 4	Educare birth to age 5	Difference
Earnings benefits	$53,000	$134,000	$81,000
Program costs	$10,000	$87,000	$77,000
Ratio of benefits to costs	5.3	1.5	1.1

NOTE: Benefits and costs are rounded to the nearest thousand, in present-value 2012 dollars. The first two columns of numbers come from Table 3.1. The third column subtracts age four pre-K benefits and costs from Educare benefits and costs.
SOURCE: Author's calculations, as explained in text and endnotes.

net benefit per child is sizable. These dollar benefits are targeted at a needy group, while the taxes would be raised from wealthier groups. In addition to these direct earnings benefits for former child participants, the extra skills from Educare will add to spillover benefits. Also, five years of full-day child care will have much higher benefits for parental earnings.

NURSE FAMILY PARTNERSHIP FOR ALL DISADVANTAGED FIRST-TIME MOTHERS

The proposal includes full funding for Nurse Family Partnership services for everyone in the program's target group, which is disadvantaged first-time mothers. The services would be income-targeted because of the research evidence that the NFP is most effective for this group.

The NFP is included because it has the most extensive research evidence for long-term benefits among parenting programs. However, local areas would be given options for experimenting with alternative parenting programs that show some evidence of success.

COSTS

This proposal's costs are presented in Table 7.2.[69] Universal pre-K is assumed to enroll 74 percent of all four-year-olds, similar to Oklahoma's program. Educare is assumed to be funded sufficiently to be open to all children under five from families below the poverty line, which is 25 percent of all children. Three-quarters of all such families are assumed to take up this offer. The NFP is assumed to be funded sufficiently to provide assistance from the prenatal period to age two for all first-time mothers whose family income is below 185 percent of the poverty line (the cutoff used in the federal school lunch program); about 44 percent of all children are below this income line, and about 30 percent of these low-income children are first-born children. Three-quarters of these first-time mothers are assumed to participate in the program.

Table 7.2 Annual National Costs of Large-Scale Early Childhood Education Proposal

	Number of children	Annual gross costs	Net costs
Universal pre-K for 4-year-olds	3.0 million	$31 billion	$25 billion
Educare, birth to 5, for poor children	3.7 million	$68 billion	$58 billion
NFP for disadvantaged first-time moms	0.9 million	$4 billion	$4 billion
Adjusted for pre-K overlap	(0.8 million)		($8 billion)
Total	6.3 million		$79 billion

NOTE: Annual costs per child are $10,050 for universal pre-K, $18,381 for full-time child-care pre-K, $4,500 for home-visiting/parenting. Net costs are lower than gross costs because of cost savings on existing early childhood programs. Cost savings for universal pre-K are $6 billion for state pre-K. Cost savings for Educare are $8 billion for Head Start and $2 billion for child care subsidies. Cost savings for the NFP are $0.4 billion in Affordable Care Act funding for home-visiting. Total costs are adjusted for overlap between pre-K services under universal pre-K versus Educare for four-year-olds below the poverty line. Number of participants is adjusted for this overlap, and for children in both home-visiting and full-time child care programs.

SOURCE: Author's calculations, as explained in text and endnotes.

Some cost offsets for these programs occur because of savings on funds currently spent on state pre-K programs, Head Start, and federal child care subsidies. In addition, there is some overlap between the programs, which would save on costs if all three programs were implemented, specifically in pre-K services for four-year-olds below the poverty line.

All three programs would cost just under $80 billion annually. Over six million children would receive services. Most costs would be for Educare, followed by universal pre-K.

How large are these costs? These costs are 2.0 percent of total combined federal, state, and local taxes; 3.1 percent of total federal taxes; and 5.6 percent of total state and local taxes.[70] This would represent a significant but feasible increase in state and local tax efforts, but it would be less of a stretch if participated in by all levels of government. The $79 billion total cost is 13 percent of what is currently spent on public K–12 education (National Center for Education Statistics 2013). Therefore, such an expenditure would represent a considerable increase, but not an outlandish increase, in what is spent on public education.

AGGREGATE BENEFITS

As suggested by previous chapters, this total expenditure of $79 billion annually would increase the present value of future earnings of former child participants by a multiple of between two and three times these program costs.[71] Spillover benefits due to peer effects and agglomeration effects might be more than double the direct effects on former child participants. Anticrime benefits might be at least as valuable as the earnings benefits. Dynamic effects of expanded early childhood education on U.S. growth rates, as well as second generation effects, would further increase these economic benefits. In the long run, this proposal is likely to be self-financing, certainly after 50 years or so. But the problem is how to finance, set up, and manage these investments in the short run and the medium run, over the next 50 years.

This proposal would also make a considerable dent in U.S. income inequality. From 1979 to 2007, the real income growth of the lowest-income quintile and the real income growth of the middle-income quintile both lagged behind the average per-household income growth.[72] Growth in average income per household is higher because it includes the extra real income growth of the highest-income quintile (including the highest 1 percent of earners), which has captured much of the long-term growth in the United States.

The income growth trends imply that for the lowest-income quintile from 1979 to 2007 to have matched the growth of average household income, its 2007 income would have to be boosted by 19 percent. For the middle-income quintile from 1979 to 2007 to have matched the growth of average household income, its income would have to be boosted by 24 percent.[73] To eliminate these gaps through increased earnings requires higher-percentage increases in earnings, as earnings are only a portion of household income. The required earnings boosts for the lowest-income quintile and the middle-income quintile both turn out, by coincidence, to equal a 31 percent boost in real earnings.[74]

What could this proposal do to counter these adverse trends in U.S. income inequality? As outlined in previous chapters, full-day pre-K might raise average earnings for the middle class by 5 percent. Therefore, by itself, universal pre-K would offset one-sixth (5 percent divided by 31 percent) of the lagging income growth of the middle class over the last 30 years. Educare from birth to age five might boost average earnings of children from low-income families by 26 percent. This would offset five-sixths (26 percent divided by 31 percent) of the lagging income growth of the lowest-income quintile over the past 30 years. To this would be added a 3 percent earnings boost from the NFP for the 30 percent of low-income children who are first-born children. Early childhood education cannot by itself permanently solve the income inequality problem, but it does make a considerable dent in offsetting recent inequality trends.

ACCOUNTABILITY AND QUALITY IMPROVEMENT

Large benefits of early childhood education depend upon high quality. The funding levels per child outlined above are sufficient for high quality, but they provide no guarantee. To check on program quality, outcomes for program participants should regularly be measured relative to a comparison group that is similar in observed and unobserved preexisting characteristics. For universal pre-K, this comparison can be done using the "regression discontinuity" methodology, as discussed in Chapter 2. Universal pre-K participants would be tested both at pre-K entrance and at kindergarten entrance. If pre-K has an impact, this should be apparent in a "jump"—a discontinuity—in test scores at the age cutoff for kindergarten entrance.

For Educare and the NFP, outcomes for program participants should be measured by comparing the targeted low-income group with similar children whose family income is slightly above the cutoff for the program. If these programs have an impact, the outcomes for children just below the income cutoff should be elevated relative to outcomes for children just above the income cutoff.

While cognitive test scores are useful for monitoring overall program quality, heavy reliance on cognitive test scores may be problematic as a tool for accountability for individual classrooms or teachers. As discussed in previous chapters, much of the impact of early childhood education comes from the program's long-run effects on social skills and character skills. The initial boost to cognitive skills is important in helping lead to these long-run effects. But the initial boost to social and character skills is also important. As discussed in Chapter 2, the initial boost to cognitive test scores tends to underpredict long-run earnings effects, which suggests that something else is going on. An accountability system for individual early-childhood teachers that relies too much on cognitive test-score gains may lead teachers to underemphasize social and character skills.

A promising alternative accountability system for individual classrooms and teachers would rely on outside observers, who would provide an objective assessment of the quality of teacher-student interactions in the early childhood classroom. Such observer ratings are predictive of test score gains. Yet most observer ratings focus not just on cognitive skills, but also on whether the classroom climate develops social and character skills. In addition, an observer rating system, compared to an accountability system based solely on cognitive test scores, provides more useful immediate feedback to teachers.

Such observer rating systems might usefully be supplemented by teacher mentors who work with classroom teachers. After an observer rating, mentors can provide teachers with advice and training on how to improve.[75]

Such observer rating systems and teacher mentoring offer promise for improving the quality of pre-K and child care programs. Observer audits and mentoring might also be used to improve the quality of home-visiting/parenting programs.

WHAT LEVEL OF GOVERNMENT SHOULD BE RESPONSIBLE FOR EARLY CHILDHOOD EDUCATION?

An important issue is how responsibility for early childhood education should be divided among federal, state, and local governments. Where possible, we should explore whether responsibility can feasibly be assigned to state and local governments, for several reasons. First, the federal government has a lot on its plate. Health care and an aging population will absorb a great deal of federal money and attention. Federal resources are limited and should be focused on program elements for which the federal government has special comparative advantages over state and local governments.

Second, the federal government can sometimes be more bureaucratic than state and local governments. Over-rigidity in government is a particular problem for early childhood education, which needs experimentation with new program designs.

For universal pre-K, state and local government responsibility for the financing of basic operations seems feasible because the benefits of universal pre-K are mostly local. Over 60 percent of all Americans spend the bulk of their working careers in the state in which they spent their early childhoods (Bartik 2011). If a state invests in universal pre-K, about three-quarters of the increased earnings from this investment will accrue to workers who stay in the state.[76]

State and local areas that outcompete other areas in offering universal pre-K may obtain some extra benefits in higher property values. Even if people do not fully understand the value of universal pre-K, we know that people value higher elementary-school test scores in the housing market, because research studies have consistently found that a similar house will sell for more if it is assigned to a school with higher test scores. From the estimated effects of higher test scores on higher property values, and the estimated effects of pre-K on higher test scores, we can estimate that universal pre-K would be expected to increase property values by at least six times the annual program costs (Bartik 2011, Table 7.3). This benefits all local property owners, not just parents, which helps broaden local support. The increased local property-tax revenues might also increase the incentive for local governments to invest in pre-K.[77]

State and local responsibility for universal pre-K also seems feasible because the cost is modest compared to current state responsibilities. The $25 billion cost of universal pre-K would add only 1.75 percent to overall state and local taxes. This cost is also only 4 percent of what is currently spent on K–12 education.[78]

The federal government may have a comparative advantage in supporting some universal pre-K components, such as the evaluation and training components described previously. What is learned from evaluating a particular program benefits the entire nation, not one state or local area. Furthermore, self-evaluation by a state of its own programs is politically challenging. Federal standards and financing for evaluation can help encourage evaluations to have greater quality and objectivity. Finally, because quality is hard to measure, there may be some political temptation for state and local governments to over-state program quality and under-invest in quality improvement. Federal financial support and standards for quality improvement can help offset this temptation. For all of these reasons, the quality of universal pre-K is likely to be improved if there is generous federal financial support for a testing-and-outside-observer evaluation system, and for teacher mentors.

For early childhood education programs that are targeted at the poor, such as Educare and the NFP, greater federal responsibility may be necessary. The interests of the poor often have limited political clout in state and local policy. Whether justified or not, state and local policymakers often fear that income redistribution may repel middle-class and upper-class state residents, while attracting lower-class residents. Educare plus the NFP would cost $62 billion annually, which is 4.4 percent of overall state and local taxes. Although this is a modest tax increase, it is a hard sell for a proposal whose direct benefits are limited to low-income families. If high-quality child care for the poor is ever to become a reality in the United States, the federal government will probably have to play a major role in providing the needed funds.

CONCLUDING COMMENTS

Research evidence supports a proposal that would provide some direct benefits from universal pre-K for all families, while providing extra services at earlier ages for low-income families. Involvement by all levels of government in financing the system can be justified. Higher quality for these programs should be promoted by adequate financial support, program monitoring, and training.

Chapter 8

Why Early Childhood Education Makes Sense Now

ECE's Place in the Ongoing Struggle for Broader Economic Opportunities

As this book has argued, high-quality early childhood education can increase U.S. economic growth and broaden opportunities. In this chapter, early childhood education is put in a larger context. Early childhood education is part of a strategy to increase the quality of the U.S. labor supply, which along with labor demand policies can increase job quality. Early childhood education builds on a history in this country of education reforms. Today's economy requires more skills, while research shows that interventions pay off at earlier ages than was once supposed.

LABOR SUPPLY AND LABOR DEMAND

To broadly increase earnings, the American economy needs to expand both the labor supply of skills and the demand for skills. Higher employment and wages require more skilled workers as well as sufficient labor demand to employ these workers at high wages. Private market forces lead to some expansion of skills supply and demand. However, throughout American history, expansion of skills supply and demand has also been pursued by government.

HISTORY MATTERS

Historically in the United States, skills supply and demand have been affected by many policies. On the labor demand side, these have included the banking system; the legal framework for limited-liability

73

corporations; infrastructure investments in canals, railroads, high-ways, and airports; antitrust regulations; and regulations of wages and working conditions.

The United States has also reformed education to enhance quality and broaden benefits to more Americans. Our education system was not set in stone by the Founding Fathers: At the time of the American Revolution and for some years thereafter, public education was limited in scope and access. Public schools charged fees to most students, although these fees might be waived for "paupers." Public education did not extend all the way to high school, let alone college.

American education changed with the "common school movement" of the nineteenth century and the "high school movement" of the late nineteenth and early twentieth centuries. The common school movement, a grassroots effort that spread from state to state, advocated universal, free public education in graded schools up through eighth grade. The high school movement advocated universal, free high school education. The United States was the world leader in pursuing education for all to such an advanced level.

THE CONTINUING ARGUMENT OVER EXPANDING EDUCATIONAL ACCESS

These education reforms were contested. Past arguments made for the common school and for high school for all can be used, with slight modifications, to argue for early childhood education today.

Horace Mann, a prominent figure in the common school movement whose changes in Massachusetts spread nationwide, made explicit that this reform was aimed at broadening economic opportunity. According to Mann, writing in 1848,

> Nothing but universal education can counterwork [the] tendency to the domination of capital and the servility of labor. . . . If education be equally diffused, it will draw property after it by the strongest of all attractions, for such a thing never did happen, and never can happen, as that an intelligent and practical body of men should be permanently poor.

For this reason, our economic theories must include education:

That political economy, therefore, which busies itself about
capital and labor, supply and demand, interests and rents,
favorable and unfavorable balances of trade, but leaves out of
account the elements of a wide-spread mental development, is
naught but stupendous folly. (Mann 1848)

Thaddeus Stevens, later an abolitionist leader in the U.S. Congress, made his reputation in the Pennsylvania state legislature by arguing that public education should be free for all, not just for "paupers." In 1835, Stevens argued that universal free access would avoid stigmatizing the poor:

The amendment which is now proposed . . . is, in my opinion, of
a most hateful and degrading character. . . . It proposes that . . .
the names of those who have the misfortune to be poor men's
children shall be forever preserved, as a distinct class, in the
archives of the county. The teacher, too, is to keep in his school
a pauper book, and register the names and attendance of poor
scholars; thus pointing out and recording their poverty in the
midst of their companions. Sir, hereditary distinctions of rank
are sufficiently odious, but that which is founded on poverty is
infinitely more so. Such a law should be entitled, "An act for
branding and marking the poor, so that they may be known from
the rich and proud." (Stevens 1835, reprinted in 1904)

Education reformers held that broader educational access was in the enlightened self-interest of most Americans. The state education department in Iowa, in 1914, argued the following:

The landlord who lives in town . . . may well be reminded that
when he offers his farm for sale it will be to his advantage to
advertise, 'free transportation to a good graded school.' Those
who have no children to attend school . . . should be interested
in securing to the children of the whole community the best edu-
cational advantages possible. . . . If they live out their years
with no children to depend upon in old age, they must of neces-
sity rely upon someone, they know not whom, who is today in

the public schools. Their only safeguard lies in giving the best advantages possible to all. (Goldin and Katz 2008, p. 193).

Expanded education was contested. In 1874, in the "Kalamazoo School Case," local property owners argued that they shouldn't have to pay taxes for a free public high school because it was unnecessary for most Americans to go to high school. But the Michigan Supreme Court, in a ruling that influenced courts throughout the United States, held that more education was of broad public benefit:

> *We must confess to no little surprise that the legislation and policy of our state were appealed to against the right of the state to furnish a liberal education to the youth of the state in schools brought within the reach of all classes. We supposed it had always been understood in this state that education, not merely in the rudiments, but in an enlarged sense, was regarded as an important practical advantage to be supplied at their option to rich and poor alike, and not as something pertaining merely to culture and accomplishment to be brought as such within the reach of those whose accumulated wealth enabled them to pay for it.* (*Stuart v. Kalamazoo School Dist.* 1874)

BUT WHY EARLY CHILDHOOD EDUCATION? AND WHY NOW?

But even if education in general is good, why expand early childhood education? What has changed that might justify this departure from longstanding tradition?

First, globalization and technological change mean that both individual prosperity, and the collective prosperity of a nation, state, or city, depend more and more upon better skills for all. Skills development must be a higher public priority, by any means that work. Among alternative means for developing skills, research support is especially strong for early childhood education.

Second, our research on child development has advanced. Earlier-age educational interventions provide more child development benefits than was once supposed.

Third, many families are under increased stress. If more families need to rely on outside child care, efforts should be increased to ensure that this care enhances educational development.

DOING THE GOOD WE KNOW HOW TO DO

Expanded early childhood education is not the only policy that could expand economic opportunities for most Americans. K–16 reforms could help, by increasing teacher quality, adding additional learning time, or making postsecondary options more affordable. Labor demand policies could help, by investing in infrastructure, providing manufacturing extension services, increasing minimum wages, and enacting lower marginal tax rates on job creation.

But early childhood education is a policy that we know can work, and that we know how to do. As outlined in this book, there is rigorous research evidence that high-quality early childhood education works in building skills and earnings. We also have ways of monitoring and improving program quality, through a combination of testing, classroom observations, and teacher mentors.

The argument can be raised that our knowledge is imperfect. More good research is needed, but skepticism can go too far. No social reform will ever have perfect evidence. Early childhood education has more evidence of short-term and long-term effectiveness than almost any other proposed intervention to broaden opportunities.

Early childhood education can make a difference, even if we do nothing else about labor supply or demand. Pre-K programs can boost children's opportunities, even if we do not solve all the problems of the K–16 system. For example, the Chicago Child-Parent Centers helped child participants to increase their adult earnings, even though the Chicago Public Schools system continues to face many challenges.

Furthermore, skills development from early childhood education will create good jobs, even without policies that directly target job creation. A metropolitan area that uses early childhood education to boost its residents' skills will attract and grow high-quality jobs.

Broadening economic opportunities for most Americans is challenging. To make progress, we need feasible policies that can make a big difference. Throughout their nation's history, Americans have sought to expand educational opportunities. A logical next step, backed by research, is expanding high-quality early childhood education.

Notes

1. State pre-K data here and following from Barnett et al. (2013). Dollar figures are in 2012–2013 dollars.
2. This book ignores recent federal proposals by President Obama and others, both because their passage is unlikely and because such discussion instantly becomes dated.
3. Unless otherwise stated, all dollar figures in this book are stated in 2012 dollars.
4. In 2012, total federal, state, and local government tax receipts plus social insurance contributions were $3,997 billion (BEA 2012).
5. The education effects are calculated based on the age 30 analysis of the Abecedarian program (Campbell et al. 2012). The earnings effects of educational improvements are calculated using data from the Current Population Survey's Outgoing Rotation Group on African American wages, employment rates, and weekly work hours for different education groups (Bartik 2011, Technical Appendix 4B). The extra employment effects are calculated by adding on 12 percent to the treatment group employment rate at age 21, and by moderating this difference to be 6 percent at ages 27 and above. Campbell et al. (2002) find employment rate effects at age 21 that are 12 percent above the predicted effect of increased education.
6. Bartik 2011, Technical Appendix 4B. The anticrime effects depend on how imprisonment and a prison record affect earnings. Test-score effects are based on correlations between test scores and adult earnings.
7. Realizing the power of random assignment requires that there be only modest problems stemming from imperfect adherence to random assignment or sample attrition. These conditions have been met for early childhood programs. For example, the benefits of Perry Preschool have survived a reexamination of the program by Heckman et al. (2010).
8. Although random assignment experiments are the "gold standard," they are difficult to do, expensive, and rare. Studies with good comparison groups due to "natural experiments" should be viewed as "silver standard" evidence, as the treatment and comparison groups are likely similar in unobserved characteristics. Studies that only have controls for observable characteristics provide "bronze standard" evidence: suggestive but possibly biased.
9. CPC's evidence is less rigorous than other natural experiments because CPC is comparing voluntary participants in CPC in treatment-group neighborhoods with a sample of all children in comparison neighborhoods, which includes both families who would have participated in CPC and others. However, this comparison is better than comparing vol-

unteers with non-volunteers, as is done in many education studies. The CPC evidence suggests that the treatment and the comparison groups are similar in observed characteristics. The CPC study is somewhere between a "silver standard" natural experiment and a "bronze standard" study that controls only for observable characteristics. However, the CPC is of great value because it is one of the few large-scale studies of pre-K with long-term evidence on adult outcomes.

10. The 8 percent estimate comes from using educational attainment to predict lifetime earnings effects (Reynolds, Temple, White, et al. 2011). Direct estimates at age 28 estimate an effect at that age of 7 percent (Reynolds, Temple, Ou, et al. 2011).

11. These studies control for observed individual characteristics in estimating how test scores predict adult earnings. Chetty et al.'s (2011) results rely on random assignment to classes with different average test-score effects for classmates, which controls for unobserved preexisting characteristics.

12. All test score predictions of adult earnings effects in this book are based on Chetty et al. (2011). A study's test score effects are first translated into change in percentiles in the overall test score distribution. Where possible, this is done using the study's information. Other times, the study only provides effect size estimates for test scores using the standard deviation in some disadvantaged group. If the study does so, this book assumes, based on Bartik, Gormley, and Adelstein (2012), that the standard deviation of test scores for the disadvantaged group is 76.5 percent of the standard deviation for all children. If no information is provided in the study on the starting test score percentile, this book assumes, based on Weiland and Yoshikawa (2013), that disadvantaged students start 0.71 standard deviations below the overall sample mean. For determining percentage earnings effects at the overall population mean, the book uses the estimated dollar and percentage effects implied by Chetty et al.'s Appendix Table V, column 1, except that these estimates are adjusted downward by the ratio of the "leave-out mean" estimates for kindergarten entrants to the ordinary least squares (OLS) estimates in Chetty et al.'s Appendix Table XIII. If the study's target group is disadvantaged children, effects are translated into percentage effects on their earnings by using updated data to do adjustments, as in Bartik, Gormley, and Adelstein (2012), for how these children's future earnings are likely to compare to average income, given their parents' income relative to average income. These updated data, based on earnings data in the American Community Survey for parents of public school first-graders, predict that children eligible for a free or reduced-price lunch will have expected adult earnings equal to 71 percent of

average earnings. Subsequent endnotes will describe this procedure as this book's standard test score prediction of earnings procedure.

13. These test score predictions differ from Bartik, Gormley, and Adelstein (2012). Their estimates assumed that the standard deviation in the disadvantaged group was equal to the standard deviation in the overall population and that the testing end score was at the median, and also predicted percentage effects at population mean earnings. This book makes more accurate assumptions.

14. This is based on Leak et al.'s (2010) end-of-treatment mean effect size of 0.28, which is assumed to be for disadvantaged groups. The earnings prediction is based on this book's standard procedure.

15. Based on Camilli et al.'s (2010) mean short-term effect size of 0.48, which is assumed to be for disadvantaged groups. The earnings prediction is based on this book's standard procedure.

16. The IHDP was targeted at low-birth-weight babies. The IHDP estimates used in this book are from Duncan and Sojourner's (2013) analysis for heavier or "high" low-birth-weight babies. They argue that these results can generate good predictions for the general U.S. population.

17. Low income is defined as less than 180 percent of the poverty line. The results for low-income children show strongly significant effects for IQ at ages two, three, five, and eight. The reading results at age eight only have a p-value of 0.216, and the math results at age eight have a p-value of 0.099. However, the reading and math test score effects are consistent in magnitude with the IQ effects at ages five and eight. Therefore, on the whole the results suggest that reading and math achievement are boosted at age eight.

18. These earnings predictions use this book's standard procedure and are based on Duncan and Sojourner's (2013) reading and math test score effects.

19. This is based on test score effects in Ladd, Muschkin, and Dodge's (2014) preferred model, column 2 of Table 4. Estimates for both reading and math are multiplied by 11 to reflect average 2009 funding. This standard deviation effect is then averaged across reading and math tests. The starting point is assumed to be the median, given that these are all-student averages. The implied percentile effect is then combined with Chetty et al. (2011) to get percentage earnings effects.

20. As discussed in Bartik, Gormley, and Adelstein (2012), each point in Figure 2.1 shows the average test score of a group of students, where students are sorted by age. This is done to make the pattern of how test scores vary with age easier to see.

21. Regression discontinuity (RD) studies of pre-K have been criticized, but these criticisms are not convincing. Whitehurst (2013b) argues that

RD estimates also reflect different parent behavior in the pre-K year. This is true, but the main difference is that parents enroll their kid in pre-K. The comparison group in RD studies is less likely to participate in pre-K than a randomly assigned control group that enters kindergarten next year. This affects the interpretation of the RD estimates: These estimates reflect effects of pre-K versus no pre-K to a greater extent than do random assignment estimates, which reflect this pre-K program versus other pre-K. But this is more of a feature than a bug if the pre-K estimates are being compared with the program's costs.

RD pre-K studies have been criticized because some children who enter pre-K will not enter kindergarten in the same school district, and therefore will be excluded from the treatment group (Armor and Sousa 2014). But this attrition could bias estimates in either direction. In addition, Bartik (2013) finds that RD estimates of pre-K's effects do not much change when we restrict estimates to the same children tested at both pre-K entrance and kindergarten entrance. Furthermore, if RD studies of pre-K are biased by attrition, this should result in a jump in other observables at the age cutoff, which is not seen in most studies. Bartik, Gormley, and Adelstein (2012) and Weiland and Yoshikawa (2013) do sensitivity tests and do not find evidence to suggest significant bias. Weiland and Yoshikawa reweight the data to correct for attrition, which makes little difference.

22. This is based on effect sizes of 0.4 to 0.6 in regression discontinuity studies (Bartik 2013, Table 1).
23. The 6-to-15-percent range is derived from the Bartik, Gormley, and Adelstein (2012) result that Tulsa's half-day program increases adult earnings of low-income children by 6 percent, and the Weiland and Yoshikawa (2013) result that earnings of low-income children will be boosted by Boston's full-day program by 15 percent. But this is consistent with other research. The average regression discontinuity effect size estimated in Wong et al. (2008), Hustedt, Barnett, and Jung (2008), and Hustedt et al. (2010) is an effect size of 0.407. Using this book's standard prediction procedure, the percentage gain in adult earnings implied by this 0.407 effect size is 7.4 percent.
24. Based on data graciously provided by Christina Weiland, the average percentile gain in test scores for free and reduced-price lunch children is 21 percentiles. This is used to predict earnings effects using this book's standard procedure.
25. Based on Tulsa (Bartik, Gormley, and Adelstein 2012). Boston estimates suggest a 15 percent earnings effect (Weiland and Yoshikawa 2013).
26. Chapter 2 and its notes explain how these estimates are based on Abecedarian and NFP estimates.

27. The $18,381 cost per year of Abecedarian/Educare is from Ludwig and Sawhill (2007), updated to 2012 prices.
28. The $10,050 figure is from Gault et al. (2008), updated to 2012 prices. A pre-K program is assumed to be six hours per day, class size of 15 children with 2 teachers, and lead teacher paid public school wages.
29. Costs from the NFP: http://www.nursefamilypartnership.org/assets/PDF/ Fact-sheets/NFP_Snapshot.
30. Future adult earnings for disadvantaged children are calculated the same as in the test score projections of earnings. The method is an updated national version of Bartik, Gormley, and Adelstein (2012). The 2012 American Community Survey is used to calculate average earnings by gender and year for all adults, and for three other groups: parents of first-graders whose family income makes them eligible for 1) a free lunch, 2) a reduced-price lunch, or 3) no lunch subsidy. As in Bartik, Gormley, and Adelstein, the average ratios of gender and age cells for these groups are projected into the future by assuming an intergenerational correlation of earnings of 0.4 (Chadwick and Solon 2002; Solon 2002). The relative weights for free-lunch versus reduced-price-lunch students are based on Tulsa pre-K enrollment. To calculate future earnings for disadvantaged children (e.g., eligible for a free or reduced-price lunch), average future earnings are multiplied by the ratio of disadvantaged children's future earnings to overall average adult earnings, which is projected to be 71.4 percent. For children from families ineligible for a free or reduced-price lunch, the projected ratio of future earnings to the overall average is estimated to be 130.1 percent. Future real earnings are assumed to increase by 1.2 percent per year, as in Bartik (2011), based on Social Security Administration projections. Future earnings and costs are discounted to age four for pre-K, age zero for Educare and the NFP. The social discount rate is the commonly used rate of 3 percent, as explained in Bartik (2011).

In subsequent endnotes, this procedure is referred to as this book's standard baseline earnings prediction procedure. For reference, the sum of career earnings in the ACS without any assumed real earnings increase or discounting is $1,556,000. With a 1.2 percent projected increase from age four, average future earnings without discounting sum to $2,584,000. With the 1.2 percent projected increase plus a 3 percent discount back to age four, discounted average future earnings are $766,000. If instead we project a 1.2 percent annual real increase from birth, average future earnings without discounting sum to $2,710,000. With a 1.2 percent annual real increase plus a 3 percent discount rate back to birth, discounted average future earnings are $714,000. For disadvantaged children these figures are multiplied by 71.4 percent.

For non-disadvantaged children, these figures are multiplied by 130.1 percent. For the benefit calculations in Table 3.1, the percentage earnings gains of 9.7 percent for full-day pre-K, 26.4 percent for Educare, and 3.2 percent for the NFP are applied to the present value of future adult earnings for disadvantaged children as of age four for pre-K, and at birth for Educare and the NFP. Cost figures are also discounted to the appropriate age for each program.

31. A half-day school-year pre-K program at age four has parental earnings benefits, in present-value terms, of 2 percent of the child's earnings benefits (Bartik 2011, p. 81). An eight-hour-per-day pre-K program for 45 weeks at age four has parental earnings benefits of 4 percent of the child's benefits (Bartik 2011, endnote 38, p. 156).

32. Murray (2013) makes two other criticisms. "The main problem is the small size of the samples [for these two programs]. . . . Another problem is that the evaluations of both Perry Preschool and Abecedarian were overseen by the same committed, well-intentioned people who conducted the demonstration projects." On the first criticism, small sample size is accounted for when standard errors are calculated. As Heckman has argued, "a small sample would actually work toward not finding anything. . . . There are methods that account for the small sample size. Size doesn't matter. It holds up" (Matthews 2013). On the second criticism, Perry and Abecedarian have been analyzed by outside researchers—Perry by Heckman et al. (2010) and Abecedarian by Barnett and Masse (2007) and Temple and Reynolds (2007).

33. Similar criticisms are made by Murray (2013), the *Wall Street Journal* (2013), Dalmia and Snell (2013), Wertheimer and Vedantam (2013), and FactCheck.org (2013).

34. Similar criticisms are made by Whitehurst (2013b) and the *Wall Street Journal* (2013).

35. Similar criticisms are made by the *Wall Street Journal* (2013).

36. Similar criticisms are made by Wertheimer and Vedantam (2013), FactCheck.org (2013), and Murray (2013).

37. The test score effects in the text are for the Peabody Picture Vocabulary test, the Woodcock Johnson III Letter-Word Identification test, and the Woodcock Johnson III Math Applied Problems test, which are the three tests administered at both the end of Head Start and the end of third grade. The source for these data is Exhibit D.1.A in the Head Start third-grade follow-up report (Puma et al. 2012). The average effect size for "treatment on the treated" is 0.217 at the end of Head Start and 0.062 at the end of third grade. If the estimates are uncorrelated, the standard error of the average effect size would be 0.065 at the end of Head Start

and 0.054 at the end of third grade. Because the estimates are probably positively correlated, these standard errors are understated. Therefore, the true effect size in third grade could be three times as great, or it could be negative: −0.06.

The earnings effects of a 0.062 effect size are predicted using this book's standard procedure. Head Start student percentage effects are based on the free lunch group only, whose future earnings are estimated to be 67.7 percent of the population mean.

38. Figure 4.1 lists only some of the test score predictions noted in Table 2.1. Figure 4.1 focuses on test score fading, and therefore only uses tests that were the same at the end of the program/beginning of kindergarten and at third grade. These are more general cognitive tests, such as IQ tests. Specific achievement tests tend not to be used at the end of preschool. Academic achievement tests give higher predictions of adult earnings than more general cognitive tests. This is part of the broadening of skills that occurs over time as children develop.

Test score effects used in the earnings predictions are as follows: CPC: Reynolds (2000), Table 9, average results for four methods controlling for selection bias from Reynolds and Temple (1995); Abecedarian: Campbell et al. (2001), IQ results from Table 1; Perry: Schweinhart et al. (2005), IQ results in Table 3.3; and Head Start test score effects come from the experiment's third-grade follow-up report, as cited in a previous endnote. Earnings predictions were done using this book's standard procedure.

Adult earnings effects based on adult outcomes for CPC come from Reynolds, Temple, White, et al. (2011); for Perry, from Heckman et al. (2010); for Abecedarian, from Campbell et al. (2012); for Head Start, from Deming (2009).

39. Gormley et al. (2010) find that the average effect size of Tulsa pre-K on literacy and math tests is over 70 percent greater than the effect size for Tulsa Head Start. Wong et al. (2008) argue that their average results from five states for various tests are about twice the average short-run effect sizes of Head Start in the recent experiment. This may exaggerate Head Start's problems, as a greater portion of the Head Start control group will enroll in an alternative pre-K program.

40. The test score effects in the Head Start experiment had considerably faded already by the end of kindergarten (end-of-kindergarten effects predict earnings effects of 1 percent, down from 4 percent at the end of the program). This rapid fading contrasts with the CPC (end-of-kindergarten test score effects predict earnings effects of 8 percent, similar to the prediction at the beginning of kindergarten) and with Abecedarian (first-grade effects predict earnings gains of 11 percent, down

from 13 percent at the end of the program). Perry also shows short-run fading, but still predicts much larger effects than Head Start (Perry has end-of-kindergarten and end-of-first-grade test score effects that predict earnings effects of 3 percent, down from 12 percent at the end of the program). Test score effects for these predictions come from the same sources cited in the endnote for Figure 4.1.

41. This book's standard prediction procedure implies that even with no real earnings increases, future average earnings will be $1,556,000.

42. Cascio and Schanzenbach's (2013) analysis of Oklahoma and Georgia concludes that the benefits of these programs will exceed costs if the programs only increase average test scores on the National Assessment of Educational Progress (NAEP) by between 1.0 and 1.4 scale points. State NAEP scores frequently jump around from one test to the next by many multiples of such amounts. This "noise"—by which is simply meant jumps in test scores due to measurement error and many random changes in state characteristics—often overwhelms plausible effects of programs.

43. This statement is based on Cascio and Schanzenbach's benefit-cost analysis using eighth-grade test scores, at a 3.4 percent discount rate, of around 3-to-1 (Table 8). Based on fourth-grade test score impacts, the benefit-cost ratio is over 7-to-1. My reanalysis of their fourth-grade results gets slightly larger benefits of over 11-to-1. This occurs because earnings effects of test scores near the mean are somewhat larger in the Chetty et al. (2011) estimates that I use than in the Chetty, Friedman, and Rockoff (2013) estimates they use. I believe Chetty et al. provides better predictions, because it links percentile gains rather than effect size gains to earnings, and Chetty et al.'s results suggest that percentile impacts are more uniformly linear across the test score distribution.

Fitzpatrick (2008) has sometimes been cited (FactCheck.org 2013, *Wall Street Journal* 2013) as showing that Georgia's program does not work, but her results suggest a benefit-cost ratio modestly greater than one for Georgia's pre-K. If one combines Fitzpatrick's assumption of a 0.09 effect size for 40 percent of Georgia's child participants in pre-K and zero effects for the other 60 percent with this book's standard test-score-to-earnings prediction procedure, the present value of earnings effects is 1.3 times costs, estimated at $3,652 in Cascio and Schanzenbach (2013). Fitzpatrick does not get this result because she assumes a fixed dollar effect of test score increases on hourly wages, which seems implausible.

44. Cascio and Schanzenbach (2013) state that the most precise test score results for fourth-grade math are only significantly different from zero at the 20 percent level.

45. A possible sign of such biases is some discrepancy between results for the smaller sample with parental consent and the full sample (Lipsey et al. 2013b). The discrepancy concerns one of the few outcomes for which parental consent is not needed, which is whether the child is retained in kindergarten. The smaller sample finds that Tennessee pre-K reduces retention in kindergarten from 6 percent to 4 percent. The full sample finds that Tennessee pre-K reduces retention in kindergarten from 8 percent to 4 percent. If Tennessee pre-K truly has no effect on a child's performance as of the end of kindergarten, it is strange that the full sample finds that the odds of retention are cut in half.

46. It is noteworthy that Tennessee's end of pre-K results, with an effect size of 0.24, imply an adult earnings effect of 4 percent, which is low for a full-day program compared to the 10 percent boost for low-income children estimated in Tulsa (Bartik, Gormley, and Adelstein 2012) and the 15 percent boost implied by results for Boston (Weiland and Yoshikawa 2013).

47. In these studies of how teacher-child interactions affect learning, differences between students are controlled for using only observable variables, which might leave some bias. However, many researchers would be inclined to believe that teacher-child interactions make a difference, because such an effect seems so plausible.

48. Based on Sabol et al. (2013). The lowest-quality level is below 2.5 on the 7-point Classroom Assessment Scoring System (CLASS) scale of teacher-child interactions, and the highest quality is 5.5 or above on the CLASS scale (see supplementary materials for Sabol et al. 2013). The five cognitive test results in Table S4 were averaged to get an average effect size increase of the highest quality "level four" versus "level one" of 0.322. The earnings effects of a 0.322 effect size increase in test scores at the end of pre-K are calculated using this book's standard procedure.

49. This is calculated by multiplying the 6 percent earnings effect by the present value of future adult earnings for children from families eligible for a free or reduced-price lunch, predicted using this book's standard procedure. The resulting present value of the 6 percent gain is around $33,000 per child, which, multiplied by 15 children per class, would come out to around $495,000.

50. For example, using the results in Burchinal, Kainz, and Cai (2011), which show an effect size for cognitive outcomes that averages 0.0833 for a one-standard-deviation increase in CLASS instructional support in a low-income sample, and using this book's standard prediction procedure, a one-standard-deviation increase in CLASS instructional support will raise earnings in this sample by 1.5 percent, which has a present value of $120,000 summed over 15 students in a class. Using results

from Keys et al. (2013) for a more mixed income sample—results that show that CLASS instructional support increases this sample's cognitive test scores by an effect size of 0.05—we find that a one-standard-deviation increase in CLASS instructional support will increase this sample's earnings by 1.1 percent, which has a present value of $131,000 summed over 15 students in a class. (The smaller percentage increase yields a larger present value because this sample's adult earnings will be more typical of the population.)

51. For example, research by Mashburn et al. (2008) and Blau and Currie (2006) suggests that structural aspects of pre-K and child care do not affect quality, while Travers and Goodson (1980) find evidence that lower class size helps improve effectiveness, and Kelley and Camilli (2007) survey evidence that stronger teacher credentials improve effectiveness. See Bartik (2011, pp. 135–140).

52. All of these programs used certified teachers. The available data on class sizes suggest they were moderate to small. Perry averaged 13 students to 2 teachers, Abecedarian 14 students to 2 teachers, and Chicago Child–Parent Center pre-K averaged 17 students to 2 teachers.

53. The increased costs are calculated by updating the figures from Table 1 in Gault et al. (2008) to 2012 dollars. As detailed in Bartik, Gormley, and Adelstein (2012), the figures in Chetty et al. (2011) suggest that a one percentile increase in test scores increases future adult earnings in dollar terms for all groups by 0.495 percent of mean overall earnings. Average future earnings are predicted using this book's standard baseline earnings prediction procedure, described in a previous endnote. The present value as of age four of these average earnings is $766,000. The $2,500 increment to costs is 0.33 percent of average earnings. Therefore, the needed percentile test score increase is 0.67 percent, which equals 0.33 percent divided by 0.495. Such a $2,500 increment to earnings would be about 0.5 percent of the present value at age four of future earnings for disadvantaged children, which is calculated to be $547,000.

54. The cost difference assumes lead teachers are paid public-school wages. Calculations are done similarly to the calculations for increased credential requirements, and they use similar sources.

55. These calculations are presented and explained in Bartik (2011, pp. 137, 152–153).

56. For Tulsa's full-day pre-K, percentile test-score gains for middle-class children are 89 percent of those for lower-income children (Bartik, Gormley, and Adelstein 2012). For half-day pre-K, the ratio is 88 percent. In Boston, percentile test-score gains for middle-class children are 71 percent of those for lower-income children (Bartik's calculations, based on Weiland and Yoshikawa 2013).

57. Table 5.1 is based on Bartik, Gormley, and Adelstein (2012). However, estimated gains and earnings figures use this book's standard baseline earnings prediction procedure.

58. These Tulsa results average results for both free and reduced-price lunch children using the same overall weights. These Tulsa results, from Bartik, Gormley, and Adelstein (2012), can be challenged because they cannot control for differences in unobserved characteristics between families that opt for half-day versus full-day pre-K. However, similar diminishing returns to a longer pre-K day are found in a random assignment experiment in New Jersey (Robin, Frede, and Barnett 2006). See Bartik (2011, p. 145) for more discussion.

59. These diminishing returns are based on the kindergarten test score effects of children in the Chicago Child-Parent Center who participated in two years versus one year (Reynolds 1995). Bartik (2011, p. 146) explains the calculations. Reynolds, Temple, White, et al. (2011) report similar diminishing returns based on an overall benefit-cost evaluation of two-year and one-year participants in CPC. Other studies are more pessimistic about the returns to adding a second year of pre-K. The supplement to Reynolds, Temple, Ou, et al. (2011) finds no evidence of any annual earnings or educational attainment differentials between the two-year group and the one-year group. Arteaga et al. (2014) also find no advantages for educational attainment or economic status between the two-year group and the one-year group. Finally, the meta-analysis in Leak et al. (2010) also suggests diminishing returns, although the extent differs with whether weights are used in the regressions. With weights, a two-year program only has an effect size larger by 0.02 than the baseline one-year program at 0.21, a 10 percent increase. Without weights, the prediction is that the two-year program will have an effect size that is higher by 0.11, about a 50 percent increase.

60. Based on Bartik, Gormley, and Adelstein (2012), but updating to 2012 national earnings using this book's standard procedure, a half-day pre-K program for children whose families are eligible for a free or reduced-price lunch will have a present value of future earnings gains of $32,742. The costs of a program with a child-to-teacher ratio of 15-to-2, paying certified teacher wages, will be $5,418 in 2012 dollars, based on Gault et al. (2008). The resulting ratio of earnings benefits to costs is 6.04. The full-day program, summarized in Chapter 2, has earnings benefits of $52,920, costs of $10,050. The net additional benefits of going from a half-day to a full-day program are $20,178, the net additional costs are $4,652, and the resulting incremental benefit-cost ratio is 4.36.

61. The review by Leak et al. (2010) is also consistent with this finding. As summarized by Duncan and Magnuson (2013, p. 115), "Analysis of the

meta-analytic database shows that . . . effect sizes were neither larger nor smaller for children who started programs at younger ages." Because these younger-age programs will have smaller class sizes, this implies lower benefit-cost ratios.

62. For an example of this perspective, see Dinesh D'Souza, as discussed in Bartik (2011, p. 319).

63. To be exact, $1,245,000 is the estimated dollar value of increased earnings from college graduation over a career without any secular wage increases or discounting. This college graduation premium is $2,168,000 with annual 1.2 percent real wage increases, and $571,000 if this $2.2 million is discounted at 3 percent annually.

64. Spillover wage benefits may not be uniform across all other groups. Moretti's estimates suggest greater nominal wage benefits for non–college graduates, while Diamond, in contrast, shows that the combined changes in local amenities and housing prices may disproportionately help college graduates. At the national scale, one would expect much of the overall increase in prices to disappear, while the effects on productivity would remain.

65. My 2011 book included some spillover effects, but I made relatively conservative assumptions that forced these spillover effects to be smaller than I now think is plausible.

66. There may also be spillover effects of local skills, not only on productivity levels but on productivity growth, as argued in Dickens and Baschnagel (2008).

67. The Chicago Child-Parent Center reduced students in special ed from 25 percent to 14 percent (Reynolds, Temple, White, et al. 2011). Perry reduced some special ed services, for mental impairment, from 35 percent to 15 percent, but increased some other special ed services. Overall years in special ed went from 5.2 years to 4.0 years (Schweinhart et al. 2005). Bagnato, Salaway, and Suen (2009) found that Pennsylvania's pre-K program reduced special ed services in the treatment group to 2.4 percent, versus 18 percent in the comparison group.

68. This averages test-score effects across five tests in Table 3 of Henry and Rickman (2007).

69. Universal pre-K costs are based on Gault et al. (2008). Annual full-time child care/pre-K costs are Abecedarian figures from Ludwig and Sawhill (2007), which in turn are based on Masse and Barnett (2002). Annual home-visiting/parenting costs per child are from the NFP (http://www .nursefamilypartnership.org/assets/PDF/Fact-sheets/NFP_Benefit _Cost.aspx). Oklahoma's state pre-K participation rate of 74 percent comes from Barnett et al. (2013). Assumptions for Educare on targeting to the poor and 75 percent take-up are the same assumptions as made by

Ludwig and Sawhill (2007). Assumptions for home-visiting/parenting are based on Isaacs (2007), who implies that 8.9 percent of all children are currently first births to families below 185 percent of the poverty line; Isaacs (2007) also assumes a 75 percent take-up rate. The number of children at each age under five comes from 2012 figures of the U.S. census.

70. Government tax figures are for 2012, from BEA (2012). "Contributions for social insurance" are included in taxes.

71. Under plausible assumptions, the direct earnings effects on former participants of the $79 billion proposal would boost the present value of earnings by $207 billion, about 2.6 times the cost. This assumes that in the universal pre-K program, 47 percent of pre-K participants will be needy children who will get the higher benefit-cost ratio of 5.3, and the other 53 percent will be middle-class children who will get a lower benefit-cost ratio of 4.7 to 1 (see Table 5.1). The current $6 billion spent on state pre-K is assumed to be split 85 percent to needy children, 15 percent to middle-class children. We then add in the incremental costs and benefits of the Educare and NFP proposals using Table 3.1.

72. The CBO classifies households into income quintiles based on before-tax income, adjusted for household size.

73. Average after-tax and transfer real income growth for all households from 1979 to 2007 was 67.5 percent, compared to 41.0 percent for the lowest-income quintile and 34.8 percent for the middle-income quintile. Dividing 1.675 by 1.41 yields 1.19, and dividing 1.675 by 1.348 yields 1.24, so the last year's income of these two groups needs to be blown up by 19 percent and 24 percent to match average overall income growth. These figures come from Supplemental Data files, Table 6, at http://www.cbo.gov/publication/43373.

74. For the average lowest-income-quintile household in 2007, total labor income was 61.1 percent of after-tax and transfer market income. So an earnings boost of 19 percent / 0.611 = 31 percent would be required to make up for lost income growth relative to the average household. For the middle-income quintile, 77 percent of those families' after-tax and transfer market income was labor income, so a labor income boost of 24 percent / 0.77 = 31 percent would be required to make up for lagging real income growth.

75. A recent review argues that "multiple recent studies suggest a highly promising route to quality in preschool education: providing support for teachers to implement evidence-based curricula and instruction through coaching and mentoring" (Yoshikawa et al. 2013, p. 15).

76. For the half-day program considered in Bartik (2011), the ratio of the present value of earnings to program costs was 2.78 from a state per-

spective, 3.79 from a national perspective. The ratio of the state benefits to the national benefits is 73 percent = 2.78 / 3.79.

77. If universal pre-K increases property values by six times annual program costs, annual property taxes raised would be 8 percent of annual program costs (Bartik 2011, Table 7.3).

78. This 4 percent figure may seem low considering that K–12 covers 13 grades and pre-K corresponds to one grade. However, consider the following: The gross cost is $31 billion, with the $25 billion net cost due to states already spending $6 billion on pre-K for four-year-olds; average public school expenditure divided by fall enrollment count in 2010–2011 was $12,048 (National Center for Education Statistics 2013), almost 20 percent more than the cost per child of universal pre-K of $10,050; the assumed enrollment in universal pre-K at age four is 3.0 million, which is well below one-thirteenth of total K–12 enrollment of around 49 million, both because of lower births in recent years and because of the assumption that only 74 percent of all students will take up universal pre-K given the presence of Head Start as well as parents choosing other alternatives.

References

Armor, David J., and Sonia Sousa. 2014. "The Dubious Promise of Universal Preschool." *National Affairs* 18(Winter): 36–49.

Arteaga, Irma, Sarah Humpage, Arthur J. Reynolds, and Judy A. Temple. 2014. "One Year of Preschool or Two: Is It Important for Adult Outcomes?" Results from the Chicago Longitudinal Study of the Child-Parent Centers. *Economics of Education Review* 40(June): 221–237.

Bagnato, Stephen J., Jennifer Salaway, and Hoi Suen. 2009. *Pre-K Counts in Pennsylvania for Youngsters' Early School Success: Authentic Outcomes for an Innovative Prevention and Promotion Initiative.* Research Results of SPECS for Pre-K Counts: An Independent Authentic Program Evaluation Research Initiative (2005–2009). 2009 Final Research Report. Pittsburgh, PA: Early Childhood Partnerships. http://www.heinz.org/ UserFiles/Library/SPECS for PKC 2009 Final Research Report 113009 .pdf (accessed March 14, 2014).

Barnett, W. Steven. 2013. *Expanding Access to Quality Pre-K Is Sound Public Policy.* New Brunswick, NJ: Rutgers, the State University of New Jersey, National Institute for Early Education Research.

Barnett, W. Steven, Megan E. Carolan, James H. Squires, and Kirsty Clarke Brown. 2013. *The State of Preschool 2013: State Preschool Yearbook.* New Brunswick, NJ: Rutgers Graduate School of Education, National Institute for Early Education Research.

Barnett, W. Steven, and Leonard N. Masse. 2007. "Comparative Benefit-Cost Analysis of the Abecedarian Program and Its Policy Implications." *Economics of Education Review* 26(1): 113–125.

Bartik, Timothy J. 2011. *Investing in Kids: Early Childhood Programs and Local Economic Development.* Kalamazoo, MI: W.E. Upjohn Institute for Employment Research.

———. 2013. "Effects of the Pre-K Program of Kalamazoo County Ready 4s on Kindergarten Entry Test Scores: Estimates Based on Data from the Fall of 2011 and the Fall of 2012." Upjohn Institute Working Paper No. 13-198. Kalamazoo, MI: W.E. Upjohn Institute for Employment Research. http:// research.upjohn.org/up_workingpapers/198 (accessed March 14, 2014).

Bartik, Timothy J., William T. Gormley Jr., and Shirley Adelstein. 2012. "Earnings Benefits of Tulsa's Pre-K Program for Different Income Groups." *Economics of Education Review* 31(6): 1143–1161.

Blau, David M., and Janet Currie. 2006. "Pre-School, Day Care, and After School Care: Who's Minding the Kids?" In *Handbook of the Economics of Education*, Vol. 2, Eric Hanushek and Finis Welch, eds. Handbooks in Economics 26. Amsterdam: North-Holland, pp. 1163–1278.

Burchinal, Margaret, Kirsten Kainz, and Yaping Cai. 2011. "How Well Do

Our Measures of Quality Predict Child Outcomes? A Meta-Analysis and Coordinated Analysis of Data from Large-Scale Studies of Early Childhood Settings." In *Quality Measurement in Early Childhood Settings*, Martha Zaslow, Ivelisse Martinez-Beck, Kathryn Tout, and Tamara Halle, eds. Baltimore, MD: Paul H. Brookes Publishing Co., pp. 11–31.

Bureau of Economic Analysis. 2012. *National Economic Accounts*. Interactive Tables: GDP and the National Income and Product Account (NIPA) Historical Tables. Washington, DC: U.S. Department of Commerce, Bureau of Economic Analysis.

Camilli, Gregory, Sadako Vargas, Sharon Ryan, and W. Steven Barnett. 2010. "Meta-Analysis of the Effects of Early Education Interventions on Cognitive and Social Development." *Teachers College Record* 112(3): 579–620.

Campbell, Frances A., Elizabeth P. Pungello, Margaret Burchinal, Kirsten Kainz, Yi Pan, Barbara H. Wasik, Oscar A. Barbarin, Joseph J. Sparling, and Craig T. Ramey. 2012. "Adult Outcomes as a Function of an Early Childhood Educational Program: An Abecedarian Project Follow-Up." *Developmental Psychology* 48(4): 1033–1043.

Campbell, Frances A., Elizabeth P. Pungello, Shari Miller-Johnson, Margaret Burchinal, and Craig T. Ramey. 2001. "The Development of Cognitive and Academic Abilities: Growth Curves from an Early Childhood Educational Experiment." *Developmental Psychology* 37(2): 231–242.

Campbell, Frances A., Craig T. Ramey, Elizabeth Pungello, Joseph Sparling, and Shari Miller-Johnson. 2002. "Early Childhood Education: Young Adult Outcomes from the Abecedarian Project." *Applied Developmental Science* 6(1): 42–57.

Cascio, Elizabeth U., and Diane Whitmore Schanzenbach. 2013. "The Impacts of Expanding Access to High-Quality Preschool Education." NBER Working Paper No. 19735. Cambridge, MA: National Bureau of Economic Research.

Chadwick, Laura, and Gary Solon. 2002. "Intergenerational Income Mobility among Daughters." *American Economic Review* 92(1): 335–344.

Chetty, Raj, John N. Friedman, Nathaniel Hilger, Emmanuel Saez, Diane Whitmore Schanzenbach, and Danny Yagan. 2011. "How Does Your Kindergarten Classroom Affect Your Earnings? Evidence from Project STAR." *Quarterly Journal of Economics* 126(4): 1593–1660.

Chetty, Raj, John N. Friedman, and Jonah E. Rockoff. 2013. "Measuring the Impacts of Teachers II: Teacher Value-Added and Student Outcomes in Adulthood." NBER Working Paper No. 19424. Cambridge, MA: National Bureau of Economic Research.

Currie, Janet, and Duncan Thomas. 2012. "Early Test Scores, School Quality, and SES: Long-Run Effects on Wage and Employment Outcomes." In *35th Anniversary Retrospective*, Solomon W. Polachek and Konstantinos

Tatsiramos, eds. Research in Labor Economics 35. Bradford, UK: Emerald Group Publishing, pp. 185–214.

Dalmia, Shikha, and Lisa Snell. 2013. "The Dispiriting Evidence on Preschool." *Wall Street Journal*, February 28. http://online.wsj.com/news/articles/SB10001424127887324662404578329873460933586 (accessed May 5, 2014)

Deming, David. 2009. "Early Childhood Intervention and Life-Cycle Skill Development: Evidence from Head Start." *American Economic Journal: Applied Economics* 1(3): 111–134.

Diamond, Rebecca. 2013. "The Determinants and Welfare Implications of U.S. Workers' Diverging Location Choices by Skill: 1980–2000." Working paper. Palo Alto, CA: Stanford University.

Dickens, William T., and Charles Baschnagel. 2008. "Dynamic Estimates of the Fiscal Effects of Investing in Early Childhood Programs." Issue Paper No. 5. Washington, DC: Partnership for America's Economic Success.

Duncan, Greg J., and Katherine Magnuson. 2013. "Investing in Preschool Programs." *Journal of Economic Perspectives* 27(2): 109–132.

Duncan, Greg J., Pamela A. Morris, and Chris Rodrigues. 2011. "Does Money Really Matter? Estimating Impacts of Family Income on Young Children's Achievement with Data from Random-Assignment Experiments." *Developmental Psychology* 47(5): 1263–1279.

Duncan, Greg J., and Aaron J. Sojourner. 2013. "Can Intensive Early Childhood Intervention Programs Eliminate Income-Based Cognitive and Achievement Gaps?" *Journal of Human Resources* 48(4): 945–968.

Duncan, Greg J., Kathleen M. Ziol-Guest, and Ariel Kalil. 2010. "Early-Childhood Poverty and Adult Attainment, Behavior, and Health." *Child Development* 81(1): 306–325.

FactCheck.org. 2013. "Obama's Preschool Stretch: The President Makes Misleading Claims in His Effort to Sell a Universal Preschool Plan." Philadelphia: Annenberg Public Policy Center. http://www.factcheck.org/2013/02/obamas-preschool-stretch/ (accessed February 28, 2014).

Fitzpatrick, Maria D. 2008. "Starting School at Four: The Effect of Universal Pre-Kindergarten on Children's Academic Achievement." *B.E. Journal of Economic Analysis and Policy* 8(1): 1–38.

Garces, Eliana, Duncan Thomas, and Janet Currie. 2002. "Longer Term Effects of Head Start." *American Economic Review* 92(4): 999–1012.

Gault, Barbara, Anne W. Mitchell, Erica Williams, Judy Dey, and Olga Sorokina. 2008. *Meaningful Investments in Pre-K: Estimating the Per-Child Costs of Quality Programs*. Washington, DC: Institute for Women's Policy Research.

Goldin, Claudia, and Lawrence F. Katz. 2008. *The Race between Education and Technology*. Cambridge, MA: Belknap Press of Harvard University Press.

Gormley, William T. Jr., Deborah Phillips, Shirley Adelstein, and Catherine Shaw. 2010. "Head Start's Comparative Advantage: Myth or Reality?" *Policy Studies Journal* 38(3): 397–418.

Greenwood, Peter W., Karyn Model, C. Peter Rydell, and James Chiesa. 1998. *Diverting Children from a Life of Crime: Measuring Costs and Benefits.* Santa Monica, CA: RAND Corporation.

Hanushek, Eric A., John F. Kain, Jacob M. Markman, and Steven G. Rivkin. 2003. "Does Peer Ability Affect Student Achievement?" *Journal of Applied Econometrics* 18(5): 527–544.

Heckman, James J. 2000. "Policies to Foster Human Capital." *Research in Economics* 54(1): 3–56.

Heckman, James J., Seong Hyeok Moon, Rodrigo Pinto, Peter A. Savelyev, and Adam Yavitz. 2010. "The Rate of Return to the High/Scope Perry Preschool Program." *Journal of Public Economics* 94(1–2): 114–128.

Henry, Gary T., and Dana K. Rickman. 2007. "Do Peers Influence Children's Skill Development in Preschool?" *Economics of Education Review* 26(1): 100–112.

Hoxby, Caroline. 2000. "Peer Effects in the Classroom: Learning from Gender and Race Variation." NBER Working Paper No. 7867. Cambridge, MA: National Bureau of Economic Research.

Hustedt, Jason T., W. Steven Barnett, and Kwanghee Jung. 2008. *Longitudinal Effects of the Arkansas Better Chance Program: Findings from Kindergarten and First Grade.* New Brunswick, NJ: National Institute for Early Education Research.

Hustedt, Jason T., W. Steven Barnett, Kwanghee Jung, and Allison H. Friedman. 2010. *The New Mexico PreK Evaluation: Impacts from the Fourth Year (2008–2009) of New Mexico's State-Funded PreK Program.* New Brunswick, NJ: National Institute for Early Education Research.

Isaacs, Julia B. 2007. *Cost-Effective Investments in Children.* Report for Budgeting for National Priorities Project. Washington, DC: Brookings Institution.

Kelley, Pamela, and Gregory Camilli. 2007. "The Impact of Teacher Education on Outcomes in Center-Based Early Childhood Education Programs: A Meta-Analysis." NIEER working paper. New Brunswick, NJ: Rutgers, the State University of New Jersey, National Institute for Early Education Research.

Keys, Tran D., George Farkas, Margaret R. Burchinal, Greg J. Duncan, Deborah L. Vandell, Weilin Li, Erik A. Ruzek, and Carollee Howes. 2013. "Preschool Center Quality and School Readiness: Quality Effects and Variation by Demographic and Child Characteristics." *Child Development* 84(4): 1171–1190.

Ladd, Helen F., Clara G. Muschkin, and Kenneth A. Dodge. 2014. "From

Birth to School: Early Childhood Initiatives and Third-Grade Outcomes in North Carolina." *Journal of Policy Analysis and Management* 33(1): 162–187.

La Paro, Karen M., Robert C. Pianta, and Megan Stuhlman. 2004. "The Classroom Assessment Scoring System: Findings from the Prekindergarten Year." *Elementary School Journal* 104(5): 409–426.

Leak, James, Greg J. Duncan, Weilin Li, Katherine Magnuson, Holly Schindler, and Hirokazu Yoshikawa. 2010. "Is Timing Everything? How Early Childhood Education Program Impacts Vary by Starting Age, Program Duration, and Time since the End of the Program." Paper presented at the 2010 Fall Research Conference of the Association for Public Policy Analysis and Management, "Making Fair and Effective Policy in Difficult Times," held in Boston, MA, November 4–6.

Lerner, Sharon. 2012. "Pre-K on the Range." *American Prospect* 23(8): 60–67.

Lipsey, Mark W., Kerry G. Hofer, Nianbo Dong, Dale C. Farran, and Carol Bilbrey. 2013a. *Evaluation of the Tennessee Voluntary Prekindergarten Program: End of Pre-K Results from the Randomized Control Design.* Nashville, TN: Vanderbilt University, Peabody Research Institute.

———. 2013b. *Evaluation of the Tennessee Voluntary Prekindergarten Program: Kindergarten and First Grade Follow-Up Results from the Randomized Control Design.* Nashville, TN: Vanderbilt University, Peabody Research Institute.

Ludwig, Jens, and Douglas L. Miller. 2007. "Does Head Start Improve Children's Life Chances? Evidence from a Regression Discontinuity Design." *Quarterly Journal of Economics* 122(1): 159–208.

Ludwig, Jens, and Isabel Sawhill. 2007. "Success by Ten: Intervening Early, Often, and Effectively in the Education of Young Children." Hamilton Project Discussion Paper 2007-02. Washington, DC: Brookings Institution.

Lynch, Robert G. 2007. *Enriching Children, Enriching the Nation: Public Investment in High-Quality Prekindergarten.* Washington, DC: Economic Policy Institute.

Mann, Horace. 1848. *Horace Mann on Education and National Welfare.* Twelfth Annual Report of Horace Mann as Secretary of Massachusetts State Board of Education. Nashville, TN: TnCrimLaw.com. http://www.tncrimlaw.com/civil_bible/horace_mann (accessed February 28, 2014).

Mashburn, Andrew J., Robert C. Pianta, Bridget K. Hamre, Jason T. Downer, Oscar A. Barbarin, Donna Bryant, Margaret Burchinal, Diane M. Early, and Carollee Howes. 2008. "Measures of Classroom Quality in Prekindergarten and Children's Development of Academic, Language, and Social Skills." *Child Development* 79(3): 732–749.

Masse, Leonard N., and W. Steven Barnett. 2002. *A Benefit Cost Analysis of the Abecedarian Early Childhood Intervention.* New Brunswick, NJ: National Institute for Early Education Research.

Matthews, Dylan. 2013. "James Heckman: In Early Childhood Education, 'Quality Really Matters.'" *Wonkblog: Economic and domestic policy, and lots of it, Washington Post,* February 14. www.washingtonpost.com/blogs/wonkblog/wp/2013/02/14/james-heckman-in-early-childhood-education-quality-really-matters/ (accessed May 6, 2014).

Moretti, Enrico. 2003. "Human Capital Externalities in Cities." NBER Working Paper No. 9641. Cambridge, MA: National Bureau of Economic Research.

———. 2004. "Estimating the Social Return to Higher Education: Evidence from Longitudinal and Repeated Cross-Sectional Data." *Journal of Econometrics* 121(1–2): 175–212.

———. 2012. *The New Geography of Jobs.* New York: Houghton Mifflin Harcourt.

Murray, Charles. 2013. "The Shaky Science behind Obama's Universal Pre-K." *Bloomberg View,* February 20. http://www.bloombergview.com/articles/2013-02-21/the-shaky-science-behind-obama-s-universal-pre-k (accessed May 8, 2014).

National Center for Education Statistics. 2013. *Digest of Education Statistics.* Washington, DC: National Center for Education Statistics.

Neidell, Matthew, and Jane Waldfogel. 2010. "Cognitive and Noncognitive Peer Effects in Early Education." *Review of Economics and Statistics* 92(3): 562–576.

Obama, Barack. 2013. "Remarks by the President on Early Childhood Education—Decatur, GA." Washington, DC: White House, Office of the Press Secretary. http://www.whitehouse.gov/the-press-office/2013/02/14/remarks-president-early-childhood-education-decatur-ga (accessed February 21, 2014).

Olds, David L., John Eckenrode, Charles R. Henderson Jr., Harriet Kitzman, Jane Powers, Robert Cole, Kimberly Sidora, Pamela Morris, Lisa M. Pettitt, and Dennis Luckey. 1997. "Long-Term Effects of Home Visitation on Maternal Life Course and Child Abuse and Neglect: Fifteen-Year Follow-Up of a Randomized Trial." *Journal of the American Medical Association* 278(8): 637–643.

Olds, David L., JoAnn Robinson, Lisa M. Pettitt, Dennis W. Luckey, John Holmberg, Rosanna K. Ng, Kathy Isacks, Karen Sheff, and Charles R. Henderson Jr. 2004. "Effects of Home Visits by Paraprofessionals and by Nurses: Age 4 Follow-Up Results of a Randomized Trial." *Pediatrics* 114(6): 1560–1568.

Puma, Michael, Stephen Bell, Ronna Cook, Camilla Heid, Pam Broene, Frank Jenkins, Andrew Mashburn, and Jason Downer. 2012. *Third Grade*

Follow-Up to the Head Start Impact Study: Final Report. OPRE Report 2012-45. Washington, DC: U.S. Department of Health and Human Services, Administration for Children and Families, Office of Planning, Research, and Evaluation.

Reynolds, Arthur J. 1995. "One Year of Preschool Intervention or Two: Does It Matter?" *Early Childhood Research Quarterly* 10(1): 1–31.

———. 2000. *Success in Early Intervention: The Chicago Child-Parent Centers.* Lincoln, NE, and London: University of Nebraska Press.

Reynolds, Arthur J., and Judy A. Temple. 1995. "Quasi-Experimental Estimates of the Effects of a Preschool Intervention: Psychometric and Econometric Comparisons." *Evaluation Review* 19(4): 347–373.

Reynolds, Arthur J., Judy A. Temple, and Suh-Ruu Ou. 2010. "Impacts and Implications of the Child-Parent Center Preschool Program." In *Childhood Programs and Practices in the First Decade of Life: A Human Capital Integration*, Arthur J. Reynolds, Arthur J. Rolnick, Michelle M. Englund, and Judy A. Temple, eds. New York: Cambridge University Press, pp. 168–187.

Reynolds, Arthur J., Judy A. Temple, Suh-Ruu Ou, Irma A. Arteaga, and Barry A. B. White. 2011. "School-Based Early Childhood Education and Age-28 Well-Being: Effects by Timing, Dosage, and Subgroups." *Science* 333(6040): 360–364.

Reynolds, Arthur J., Judy A. Temple, Barry A. B. White, Suh-Ruu Ou, and Dylan L. Robertson. 2011. "Age 26 Cost-Benefit Analysis of the Child-Parent Center Early Education Program." *Child Development* 82(1): 379–404.

Robin, Kenneth B., Ellen C. Frede, and W. Steven Barnett. 2006. *Is More Better? The Effects of Full-Day vs. Half-Day Preschool on Early School Achievement.* New Brunswick, NJ: Rutgers, the State University of New Jersey, National Institute for Early Education Research.

Sabol, Terri J., Sandra L. Soliday Hong, Robert C. Pianta, and Margaret R. Burchinal. 2013. "Can Rating Pre-K Programs Predict Children's Learning?" *Science* 341(6148): 845–846.

Schweinhart, Lawrence J., Jeanne Montie, Zongping Xiang, William S. Barnett, Clive R. Belfield, and Milagros Nores. 2005. *Lifetime Effects: The High/Scope Perry Preschool Study through Age 40.* Ypsilanti, MI: HighScope Educational Research Foundation.

Solon, Gary. 2002. "Cross-Country Differences in Intergenerational Earnings Mobility." *Journal of Economic Perspectives* 16(3): 59–66.

Stevens, Thaddeus. (1835) 1904. *The Famous Speech of Hon. Thaddeus Stevens of Pennsylvania: In Opposition to the Repeal of the Common School Law of 1834, in the House of Representatives of Pennsylvania, April 11, 1835.* Reprint, Philadelphia: Thaddeus Stevens Memorial Association of Philadelphia.

Stuart v. Kalamazoo School Dist. 1874. 30 Mich. 69 (1874).

Temple, Judy A., and Arthur J. Reynolds. 2007. "Benefits and Costs of Investments in Preschool Education: Evidence from the Child–Parent Centers and Related Programs." *Economics of Education Review* 26(1): 126–144

Travers, Jeffrey, and Barbara Dillon Goodson. 1980. *Research Results of the National Day Care Study.* Final Report of the National Day Care Study, Vol. 2. Prepared for the Department of Health, Education, and Welfare. Cambridge, MA: Abt Associates.

U.S. Department of Health and Human Services. 2010. *Head Start Impact Study.* Final Report. Washington, DC: Department of Health and Human Services, Administration for Children and Families, Office of Planning, Research, and Evaluation.

Wall Street Journal. 2013. "Review and Outlook: Head Start for All." Editorial. *Wall Street Journal,* February 27.

Weiland, Christina, and Hirokazu Yoshikawa. 2013. "Impacts of a Pre-kindergarten Program on Children's Mathematics, Language, Literacy, Executive Function, and Emotional Skills." *Child Development* 84(6): 2112–2130.

Wertheimer, Linda, and Shankar Vedantam. 2013. "Is the Call for Universal Pre-Kindergarten Warranted?" Interview for radio broadcast, February 18, National Public Radio program "Morning Edition." http://www .npr.org/2013/02/18/172298073/is-the-call-for-universal-pre -kindergarten-warranted (accessed May 8, 2014).

Whitehurst, Grover J. 2013a. "Can We Be Hard-Headed about Preschool? A Look at Head Start." *The Brown Center Chalkboard* (blog), Brookings Institution, January 16. http://www.brookings.edu/blogs/brown-center -chalkboard/posts/2013/01/16-preschool-whitehurst (accessed April 24, 2013).

———. 2013b. "Can We Be Hard-Headed about Preschool? A Look at Universal and Targeted Pre-K." *The Brown Center Chalkboard* (blog), Brookings Institution, January 23. http://www.brookings.edu/blogs/brown -center-chaldboard/posts/2013/01/23-prek-whitehurst (accessed April 24, 2013).

———. 2013c. "New Evidence Raises Doubts on Obama's Preschool for All." *The Brown Center Chalkboard* (blog), Brookings Institution, November 20. http://www.brookings.edu/blogs/brown-center-chalkboard/ posts/2013/11/20-evidence-raises-doubts-about-obamas-preschool-for -all-whitehurst (accessed May 9, 2014).

Wong, Vivian C., Thomas D. Cook, W. Steven Barnett, and Kwanghee Jung. 2008. "An Effectiveness-Based Evaluation of Five State Pre-Kindergarten Programs." *Journal of Policy Analysis and Management* 27(1): 122–154.

Yoshikawa, Hirokazu, Christina Weiland, Jeanne Brooks-Gunn, Margaret R. Burchinal, Linda M. Espinosa, William T. Gormley, Jens Ludwig, Katherine A. Magnuson, Deborah Phillips, and Martha J. Zaslow. 2013. *Investing in Our Future: The Evidence Base on Preschool Education.* Ann Arbor, MI: Society for Research in Child Development; New York: Foundation for Child Development.

Author

Timothy J. Bartik is a senior economist at the W.E. Upjohn Institute for Employment Research. His research focuses on state and local economic development and local labor markets. This research includes studies of how taxes and public services, such as education, affect local and national economies.

Bartik is recognized as a leading scholar on state and local economic development policies in the United States. His 1991 book, *Who Benefits from State and Local Economic Development Policies?*, is widely cited as an important and influential review of the evidence on how local policies affect economic development. Bartik is coeditor of *Economic Development Quarterly*, the only journal focused on local economic development in the United States, and also serves on the editorial board of other regional economics journals.

Bartik's 2011 book, *Investing in Kids: Early Childhood Programs and Local Economic Development*, argues that early childhood programs can be a cost-effective complement to business tax incentives in promoting local economic development. According to Nobel Prize–winning economist James Heckman, "Tim Bartik has written a thoughtful book on the value of a local approach to financing and creating early interventions to foster child development." According to Michael Mandel, former chief economist for *BusinessWeek*, "Bartik's book is a comprehensive and compelling argument for a one-two economic development punch: how state and local governments need to combine both tax incentives for businesses and investments in early childhood education."

Bartik's other recent research includes: "The Kalamazoo Promise Scholarship," *Education Next*, 2014 (with Marta Lachowska); "The Future of State and Local Economic Development Policy: What Research Is Needed," *Growth and Change*, 2012; and "Earnings Benefits of Tulsa's Pre-K Program for Different Income Groups," *Economics of Education Review*, 2012 (with William Gormley and Shirley Adelstein).

Bartik's blog, http://investinginkids.net/, provides regular coverage of new research and public debate over early childhood programs and the economy. His Twitter account is @TimBartik.

Bartik received both his PhD and his MS in economics from the University of Wisconsin–Madison in 1982. He earned a BA from Yale University in political philosophy in 1975. Prior to joining the Upjohn Institute in 1989, he was an assistant professor of economics at Vanderbilt University. From 2000 to 2008, Bartik served on the Kalamazoo Public Schools Board of Education.

Index

The italic letters *f, n,* or *t* following a page number indicate a figure, note, or table on that page. Double letters mean more than one such item on a single page.

Abecedarian Project
  adult increase in earnings after, 23, 24*f,* 50
  age of, criticized as irrelevant today *vs.* recent studies, 30–31, 84*n*32
  benefits *vs.* costs of, 25–26, 25*t,* 49, 83–84*n*30
  child care services of, 3–4, 15
  costs of, 23, 49, 83*nn*27–28
  as model for full-time early childhood education (ECE) for disadvantaged strategy, 61, 63–64
  as random assignment study, 10–11, 79*n*5
  structural quality of, 43, 88*n*52
  test score effects and, 32–33, 33*f,* 85*n*38, 85–86*n*40
ACA (Affordable Care Act), 3
Adults, 32
  benefits *vs.* costs of earnings increases for, 24–27, 25*t,* 83–84*n*30
  earnings increases for, as ECE benefit, 1, 4, 26–27, 42, 45, 59, 87*n*49
  evidence that ECE affects outcomes for, 4, 5, 7, 9–20, 87–88*n*50
Advantaged families and ECE, 2, 6, 62
  children's benefits vary by program type, 44–47, 47*t*
Affordable Care Act, NFP expanded by, 3
Agglomeration economies, job skills competition in, 55–56
Antitrust regulations, U.S. labor demand policy and, 74

Banking system, U.S., 73
Bias, credibility and, 17, 37–38, 87*n*45
Buffett Early Childhood Fund, 4

Business investment
  infrastructure as, and U.S. labor demand policy, 73–74, 77
  new technology as, with job skills increase, 4, 54–55

Character skills, 2, 5, 33
Child Care and Development Fund, as federal block grant, 4
Child care services
  benefits of, limited to disadvantaged families, 44, 46–47
  costs of, 6, 48, 62, 66
  proposal for developmental, from birth, 7, 51, 77, 79*nn*3–4
  quality levels of, 47, 49
  as type of ECE with parental benefits, 2, 3–4, 15, 16, 26
  See also Full-time ECE for disadvantaged strategy
Child-Parent Center (CPC), Chicago
  as large-scale project with long-run earnings benefits, 30, 48, 77, 89*n*59
  long-term studies and good comparison groups with, 11, 12–13, 79–80*n*9, 80*n*10
  as model for full-day universal pre-K strategy, 3, 63
  special education costs reduced by, 58, 90*n*67
  structural quality of, 43, 88*n*52
  test score effects and, 32–33, 33*f,* 85*n*38, 85–86*n*40
Children
  age of, determines school entry level, 17–19, 19*f*
  disadvantaged, and future adult earnings, 25*t,* 47*t,* 59, 83–84*n*30, 89*n*57

Children, *cont.*
  future life course of, and ECE, 4,
    5–6, 77
  low-income, and math and reading
    scores, 81*nn*17–19, 87–88*n*50
  middle-class, benefits vary by ECE
    program type, 44–47, 47*t*
Children (under age three)
  child care services for, 4, 15–16, 47
  NFP and, 3, 43
Children (under age five)
  brain malleability in, 5, 50
  future earnings of, after ECE, 25–26,
    43–44, 46–47, 47*t*, 50–51, 88*n*53,
    88*n*55, 89*n*57
  low-income, and ECE, 6–7, 25,
    44–47, 79*nn*3–4
  middle-income, and ECE, 45–47
  skills development in, 2, 5, 50, 59
  state pre-K participants as, 3, 4, 16
Civic life, adults after ECE and, 4
Class size
  adult earnings after ECE, 43–44,
    88*n*53, 88*n*55
  costs and, 43–44, 88*nn*53–54, 89–
    90*n*61
  part of ECE structural quality, 42–43,
    88*nn*51–52
Cognitive skills, 35
  development of, in education, 2, 5
  effective, dependent on noncognitive
    skills in pre-K, 33–34
  math and reading scores, 15, 36,
    81*nn*17–19
  test scores of, *vs.* outside observers
    for classroom-teacher
    accountability, 68–69, 77
Common school movement, as
    elementary education reform,
    74–76
Community colleges, 77
Competition, 35, 53
  productivity and firms in, 55–56
CPC, Chicago. *See* Child-Parent Center,
    Chicago
Credibility
  bias minimized for, 37–38, 87*n*45
  controlled studies and, 22*f*, 87*n*47

earnings evidence, for ECE effects,
    9–10
  good comparison groups, 11–16, 31,
    79*n*8
  long-term studies and, 11–13
  randomized studies and, 10–11, 31,
    38, 79*n*7
  regression discontinuity evidence,
    17–19, 19*f*, 82*n*22
Crime reduction
  lower justice costs and, as ECE social
    benefits, 4, 57, 58, 66
  NFP and, 11, 79*n*6

Dalmia, Shikha, as ECE critic, 29,
    35–36, 84*n*33
Disadvantaged families, 19
  children age four in, and future
    earnings after ECE, 25–26
  federal support for ECE targeted to,
    2–3, 71
  free or reduced-price lunch for, and
    earnings calculations, 83*n*30,
    85*n*37, 87*n*49
  proposal for, 6–7, 79*nn*3–4
  services to, 3, 11, 16, 46, 47, 75,
    82*n*24

Early childhood education (ECE)
  accountability for high quality of,
    68–69, 77, 91*n*75
  adult outcomes of, 4, 5, 7, 9–20,
    87–88*n*50
  benefits and costs of, depend on
    program design, 7, 41–51, 62
  economic perspective on, 1–2, 8,
    51–56, 78
  effects on parents, 26, 47, 49–50, 51,
    64, 84*n*31
  evidence for, and its criticisms
    analyzed, 7, 19, 29–39
  proposals for, 6–7, 66–67, 69–71,
    79*nn*3–4
  (*see also specifics, i.e.,* First-
    time parenting for disadvantaged
    strategy; Full-day universal
    pre-K strategy; Full-time ECE
    for disadvantaged strategy)

Early childhood education (ECE), *cont.*
    public programs for, 2–4, 8
    types of (*see* Child care services;
        Parenting programs; Preschool
        education)
Earnings
    adult, increases as ECE benefit *vs.*
        costs, 1, 4, 7, 23–27, 24*f*, 25*t*, 66,
        82*nn*24–26, 91*n*71
    calculation of, for disadvantaged
        families, 27, 83–84*n*30, 87*n*49
    career, for average American worker,
        36, 86*n*41
    credibility of evidence for ECE
        effects on, 9–13
    evidence for, effects of ECE, 9–20,
        45, 87–88*n*50
    evidence with good comparison
        groups, 15–19
    long-term, predictions from short-
        term score effects, 13–15, 14*t*,
        80*n*11, 80–81*n*12, 81*nn*13–15
    summary of evidence for, 19–20
    See also Wages
ECE. *See* Early childhood education
Economic future
    cost-effective approaches to, 2, 6
    human investment and, 49, 73–78,
        89–90*n*61
    improvement of U.S., 1, 4, 8, 76, 78
    universal access to pre-K in, 1, 4, 8,
        62
Educare program
    adult increase in earnings after, 23,
        24*f*, 26, 50
    benefits *vs.* costs of, 25–26, 25*t*, 49,
        63–64, 63*t*, 83–84*n*30
    child care and pre-K services in, 4,
        10, 31
    costs of, 23, 83*nn*27–28
    as model for full-time ECE for
        disadvantaged strategy, 61,
        63–64
Education, 2, 4
    American, reform history and market
        forces, 7, 74–76
    child's, and appropriate interventions,
        5, 6, 49–51, 77, 89–90*n*61

college degrees and effect on area
    wages, 54, 55*f*, 90*nn*63–64
contemporary reform of American,
    programs, 76–78
peer effects in, as spillover benefit of
    ECE, 53, 56–57
universal free access to, 74–76
    (*see also* Universal ECE;
    Universal pre-K)
See also Special education
Employability, skills and, 33, 52*f*

FactCheck.org, repeated ECE criticism
    by, 29, 84*n*33, 84*n*36
Families
    ECE benefit for, 1, 2, 4
    See also Advantaged families;
        Disadvantaged families
Federal government
    budgets, and ECE spillover benefit
        to, 1, 58
    help to states from, 3, 4, 79*n*2
    pre-K programs of, 2–3, 36, 39
    standards evaluation as role of, 70–71
First-time parenting for disadvantaged
        strategy
    costs, 64–66, 65*t*, 69–70*n*69
    government roles in, 71
    NFP as model for, 61, 64, 68
Florida, pre-K in, 3
Full-day universal pre-K strategy, 61–63
    costs, 64–66, 65*t*, 90*n*68
    multiple models for, 63
    peer effect on test scores and, 62
Full-time ECE for disadvantaged strategy
    costs, 64–66, 65*t*, 90*n*68
    Educare/Abecedarian as model for,
        61, 63–64, 68
    government roles in, 71

Georgia, pre-K in, 3, 29, 35–37
Governments
    divided responsibility among, for
        ECE, 69–71
    intervention by, 5, 53, 73–74, 90*n*62
    levels of (*see* Federal government;
        Local government; State
        government)

Governments, *cont.*
   tax receipts of, 7, 79*n*4

Head Start program, 35, 66
   criticism of, research as statistically
      insignificant, 29, 31–35, 33*f,*
      85*n*38
   long-term studies with good
      comparison groups, 11–12
   Oklahoma with both, and close-to-
      universal pre-K, 3, 85*n*39
   as pre-K education, 2–3, 62
   test score effects and, 32–33, 33*f,*
      84–85*n*37, 85*n*38, 85–86*n*40
Heckman, James, 3, 79*n*7, 84*n*32
High school movement, as secondary
   education reform, 74, 76
HighScope Educational Research
   Foundation, Perry Preschool
   follow-up data and, 3
Home-visiting programs, 3, 10, 49–50
Human investment
   as cost-effective crime prevention,
      57, 66
   positive economic returns of, 49, 60,
      73–78, 89–90*n*61
   time and, 5–6, 58–59, 66

IHDP (Infant Health and Development
   Program), 15, 46, 81*n*16
Illinois, education in
   Chicago, and successful pre-K, 31,
      38
   Chicago CPC (*see* Child-Parent
      Center, Chicago)
Income inequality, ECE proposal would
   offset, 7, 67, 91*nn*72–74
Income levels
   low-income, 64, 81*n*17
      (*see also under* Children [under
      age 5]; Disadvantaged families;
      Lunch subsidies)
   middle-income (*see under*
      Advantaged families; Children
      [under age 5])
   parental, 26, 59
   proposals targeted by, 2–3, 51, 71

Infant Health and Development Program
   (IHDP)
   benefits limited to low-income
      families, 46
   low-birth-weight babies and, 81*n*16
   as random assignment experiment, 15
Iowa, education in, 3, 75–76
IQ, low-income effects on children's,
   81*n*17

Job skills
   American education reform and, 4, 7,
      73–78
   increased, with increased wages, 4,
      53–56, 60

Kalamazoo School Case, state supreme
   court ruling on, 76
Kindergarten, child performance and, 17,
   44–45, 57, 68, 88*n*56

Labor force
   earnings data, 36, 79*n*5, 86*n*41
   ECE benefit for, 1, 4
   job skills and wages of, 53–56, 60
   supply and demand for, 73, 77
Local government
   ECE spillover benefits to, 1, 8, 56,
      58, 90*n*66
   universal pre-K oversight by, 70,
      92*nn*77–78
Lunch subsidies, 64
   free or reduced-price, and earnings
      calculations, 83*n*30, 85*n*37,
      87*n*49, 89*n*60
   pre-K test scores with and without,
      44–45, 88*n*56

Mann, Horace, education reform and,
   74–75
Massachusetts, education in
   Boston, adult earnings after pre-K in,
      38, 87*n*46
   Boston, as model for full-day
      universal pre-K strategy, 63
   Boston, pre-K test scores in, 17,
      18–19, 45, 82*nn*24–25, 88*n*56

Massachusetts, education in, *cont.*
  Boston, successful public pre-K in,
    31, 43, 88*n*2
  reform of, 74–75
Mentoring, classroom-teacher
  accountability and, 69, 77
Michigan, education in
  Kalamazoo, 17, 76
  Ypsilanti (*see* Perry Preschool
    Program)
More at Four, aka North Carolina pre-K,
  16, 81*n*19
Murray, Charles, as ECE critic, 29, 30,
  84*nn*32–33, 84*n*36

National Public Radio, Shankar
  Vedantam repeated criticism of
  ECE on, 29
New Jersey, pre-K *vs.* kindergarten entry
  tests in, 17
New Mexico, pre-K *vs.* kindergarten
  entry tests in, 17
NFP. *See* Nurse Family Partnership
North Carolina
  child care services in, 3–4, 16
  state pre-K in, 16, 81*n*19
Nurse Family Partnership (NFP)
  adult earnings increases after, 23, 24*f,*
    26, 82*n*26
  benefits *vs.* costs of, 25–26, 25*t,* 49,
    83–84*n*30
  costs of, 23–24, 50, 83*n*29
  crime reduction with, 11, 79*n*6
  effect on parents, 26, 47, 49–50,
    84*n*31
  home visits in, 3, 10–11, 23, 49–50
  as model for first-time parenting for
    disadvantaged strategy, 61,
    64–66, 65*t,* 90–91*n*68
  as random assignment study, 10, 43,
    79*n*6

Obama, President, state pre-K under,
  36, 79*n*2
Oklahoma, pre-K in, 3
  Tulsa, adult earnings after, 38, 48,
    87*n*46, 89*n*58

Tulsa, as model for full-day universal
    pre-K strategy, 63, 64
  Tulsa, successful public-school, 31,
    43, 88*n*52
  Tulsa, test scores and universal, 17–
    18, 19*f,* 45, 81*n*20, 81–82*n*21,
    82*n*23, 82*n*25, 88*n*56
  universal, and research criticism, 29,
    35–37
Ounce of Prevention Fund, 4

Parenting programs, 2, 51
  benefits of, limited to disadvantaged
    families, 44, 46, 47, 50–51
  costs of, 49–50
  home visits in implementation of, 3
    (*see also* Nurse Family
    Partnership [NFP])
Parents, 50, 59
  ECE effects on, 26, 51, 64, 84*n*31
Pennsylvania, education in, 75, 90*n*67
Perry Preschool Program, 58, 79*n*7
  age of, criticized as irrelevant today
    vs. recent studies, 30–31, 84*n*32
  as model for full-day universal pre-K
    strategy, 63
  1960s, supported by federal funds,
    2–3, 10, 11
  structural quality of, 43, 88*n*52
  test score effects and, 32–33, 33*f,*
    85*n*38, 85–86*n*40
Pre-K (prekindergarten) education. *See*
  Preschool education
Preschool education
  benefits of, to variety of income
    groups, 44–47, 47*t,* 88*n*56, 89*n*57
  child performance upon entry into,
    vs. kindergarten, 17, 68
  cost of high-quality, 6, 45, 49, 50, 62
  cost of state, programs, 3, 16, 79*n*1
  data combined on, to minimize
    uncertainty, 36–37, 39, 86*nn*42–
    44
  duration of, and fading returns, 48,
    89*nn*58–60
  parental earnings and, 26, 84*n*31
  recent benefit-cost ratio for, 30–31,
    49–51, 63*t,* 89–90*n*61

Preschool education, *cont.*
    skills development in, and adult
        earnings, 33–34, 48
    as type of ECE, 1, 2–3
    See also Universal Pre-K
Productivity
    competitive advantage and, 55–56
    economic, as ECE spillover benefit,
        4, 53, 90n64
Public policy, U.S., on skills supply and
    demand, 73–74, 77–78
Public services, 4
    education among, funded by
        government, 2, 43, 44, 88n54
    large-scale, as problematic today,
        29–31, 39

Quality evaluation, 4, 35
    accountability for high-, of ECE,
        68–69, 77, 91n75
    benefit-cost comparison and, 1, 8, 25,
        45–46
    cost per child and, 38, 45, 87n46
    ECE and, 2, 29
    governmental financing for, 69–71
    teacher-child interactions in, 41–42,
        87nn47–48

Research criticism and ECE benefits, 7,
    19, 27, 29–39
    Head Start statistically insignificant,
        31–35
    lackluster success of state universal
        pre-K, 35–37
    old age and small size of
        experiments, 29–31
    pre-K test score effects quickly fade,
        37–39

Self-interest, enlightened, 53–54, 56–57,
    75–76
Skills development, 1
    earnings and, 33, 77
    making up deficiencies in, 48, 57
    noncognitive (*see* Character skills;
        Social skills)
    types of, in education, 2, 5

Smart Start program, child care services
    in, 15, 16
Snell, Lisa, as ECE critic, 29, 35–36,
    84n33
Social benefits, 47
    criticism of, and state pre-K, 4, 7, 27,
        35–36, 53–60
Social skills
    development of, in education, 2, 5,
        50, 57
    employability and, 33, 52f
South Carolina, pre-K *vs.* kindergarten
    entry tests in, 17
Special education, cost reduction as ECE
    spillover benefit for, 58, 90n67
Spillover effects of ECE, 53–60
    as benefits, 1, 4, 52f, 56, 58–59,
        90n65
    crime reduction, 4, 57, 58, 66
    economic productivity as, 4, 53
    government budgets and, 1, 58–59
    job skills and wages, 53–56
    next generation and, 53, 59
    peer effects in education as, 53, 56–57
State government
    budgets, and ECE spillover benefit
        to, 1, 58
    help to, and federal funds, 3, 79n2
    pre-K programs run in 40 states, 3, 8,
        37–39, 62, 66
    universal pre-K oversight by, 70,
        91–92n76, 92nn77–78
Stevens, Thaddeus, education reform
    and, 75
Structural quality, 63
    ECE affected by, 42–44, 88nn51–55
Stuart v. Kalamazoo School Dist., state
    supreme court ruling on, 76

Taxes, 77
    fiscal benefits and, 58–59
    percentage of, to fund proposed ECE
        strategies, 66, 71, 91n70
    total, 2012 receipts by governments,
        7, 79n4
    use of, justified by ECE benefits, 8,
        53, 56–57

Teacher credentials
    adult earnings after ECE and, 43–44,
        88*n*55
Teacher credentials, *cont.*
    costs and, 43–44, 88*nn*53–54
    part of ECE structural quality, 42–43,
        88*nn*51–52
Technology investment, increased job
        skills and, 4, 54–55
Tennessee, pre-K in, 17, 44
    criticism of test-score effects research
        on, 29, 37–39, 87*nn*45–46
Test scores
    adult earnings inferred from, 15, 31,
        42, 81*n*18, 87*nn*48–49, 87–88*n*50
    analytical results uncertain for small
        sample sizes, 36, 38–39, 86*n*42
    classroom-teacher accountability and,
        68–69, 77
    peer effect on, 62, 90*n*68
    short-term effects of, 29, 31, 37–39,
        84–85*n*37
    universal pre-K, in Tulsa and Boston,
        45, 88*n*56
Texas, pre-K in, 3

United States (U.S.)
    improvement of economic future in,
        1, 4, 8, 73–78
    skills supply and demand policies in,
        73–74
Universal ECE, 2, 3
    proposal for, 6–7, 51, 79*nn*3–4
Universal pre-K, 58
    criticism of state, programs, 29,
        35–37
    as model for full-day universal
        pre-K strategy, 61–63
    test scores in Tulsa and Boston,
        programs, 45, 88*n*56

Vedantam, Shankar, as ECE critic,
        84*n*33, 84*n*36
Vermont, pre-K in, 3

Wages
    education level and, 90*nn*63–64
    job skills and, 53–56, 60

regulations on, as U.S. labor demand
        policy, 74, 77
Wall Street Journal (newspaper),
    editorial criticism of ECE in, 29,
        32, 36, 84*nn*34–35
War on Poverty, 2, 81*n*17
    free- or reduced-price lunch in,
        83–84*n*30
    poverty line in, and children, 45–46,
        59, 64, 66
    (*see also* Children, low-income;
        Disadvantaged families)
Welfare reform, 4, 58
Wertheimer, Linda, interviewing Shankar
        Vedantam on ECE, 84*n*33, 84*n*36
West Virginia, pre-K in, 3, 17
Whitehurst, Russ, as ECE critic, 29, 30,
        32, 37, 39, 84*n*34
Wisconsin, pre-K in, 3
Working population. *See* Labor force

About the Institute

The W.E. Upjohn Institute for Employment Research is a nonprofit research organization devoted to finding and promoting solutions to employment-related problems at the national, state, and local levels. It is an activity of the W.E. Upjohn Unemployment Trustee Corporation, which was established in 1932 to administer a fund set aside by Dr. W.E. Upjohn, founder of The Upjohn Company, to seek ways to counteract the loss of employment income during economic downturns.

The Institute is funded largely by income from the W.E. Upjohn Unemployment Trust, supplemented by outside grants, contracts, and sales of publications. Activities of the Institute comprise the following elements: 1) a research program conducted by a resident staff of professional social scientists; 2) a competitive grant program, which expands and complements the internal research program by providing financial support to researchers outside the Institute; 3) a publications program, which provides the major vehicle for disseminating the research of staff and grantees, as well as other selected works in the field; and 4) an Employment Management Services division, which manages most of the publicly funded employment and training programs in the local area.

The broad objectives of the Institute's research, grant, and publication programs are to 1) promote scholarship and experimentation on issues of public and private employment and unemployment policy and 2) make knowledge and scholarship relevant and useful to policymakers in their pursuit of solutions to employment and unemployment problems.

Current areas of concentration for these programs include causes, consequences, and measures to alleviate unemployment; social insurance and income maintenance programs; compensation; workforce quality; work arrangements; family labor issues; labor-management relations; and regional economic development and local labor markets.

113

CPSIA information can be obtained at www.ICGtesting.com
Printed in the USA
BVOW09s1948280914

368495BV00005B/9/P

9 780880 994828